FISH of the ATLANTIC

Acknowledgments

To good fishermen everywhere.

Much of the material in this book was taken from *Anglers' Guides to the United States Atlantic Coast,* by Bruce L. Freeman and Lionel A. Walford, published by the United States Department of Commerce, National Oceanic and Atmospheric Administration, and National Marine Fisheries Service.

Cover Photo Credits: Al Ristori, Ernest Carosella

FISH
of the
ATLANTIC

by Ed Ricciuti

ISBN 0-88839-155-2
Copyright © 1982 Edward R. Ricciuti

Cataloging in Publication Data

Main entry under title:

Fish of the Atlantic

1. Marine fishes—Atlantic coast (North America)   I. Ricciuti, Edward R.
QL621.5.F58   597.092'14   C82-091162-3

All rights reserved. No part of this publication may be reproduced, stored in a retrieval system or transmitted, in any form or by any means, electronic, mechanical, photocopying, recording, or otherwise, without the prior written permission of Hancock House Publishers.

Printed in China

Editor: Donna Barne
Layout: Elizabeth McLenehan
Production & Cover Design: Peter Burakoff

Published simultaneously in Canada and the United States by

HANCOCK HOUSE PUBLISHERS LTD.
19313 Zero Avenue, Surrey, B.C. V4P 1M7
(604) 538-1114   Fax (604) 538-2262

HANCOCK HOUSE PUBLISHERS
1431 Harrison Avenue, Box X-1, Blaine, WA 98231
(206) 354-6953   Fax (604) 538-2262

Table of Contents

Introduction 6
Fish Families 8
BASSES, SEA & GROUPERS
Striped Bass 8
White Perch 9
Black Sea Bass 10
Rock Sea Bass 11
Red Grouper 12
Warsaw Grouper 13
Gag Grouper 14
Speckled Hind 15
Jewfish 16
Black Grouper 17
Nassau Grouper 18

BLUEFISH
Bluefish 19

COD, HAKES, & POLLOCK
Atlantic Cod 20
Pollock 21
Haddock 22
White Hake 23
Squirrel Hake 24
Cusk 25
Atlantic Tomcod 26
Silver Hake 27

EEL
Eel 28

DRUMS
Gray Sea Trout 29

Northern Kingfish 30
Spot 31
Silver Perch 32
Spotted Sea Trout 33
Red Drum 34
Black Drum 35
Atlantic Croaker 36
Southern Kingfish 37
Silver Sea Trout 38
Gulf Kingfish 39

BILLFISHES
White Marlin 40
Blue Marlin 41
Atlantic Sailfish 42

FLOUNDERS
Winter Flounder 43
Smooth Flounder 44
Atlantic Halibut 45
Northern Fluke 46
Windowpane 47
Southern Fluke 48

HERRING & SHAD
American Shad 49
Hickory Shad 50

MACKERELS, TUNAS, & BONITOS
Atlantic Mackerel 51
Chub Mackerel 52
Bluefin Tuna 53
Atlantic Bonito 54

Little Tuna..................55
Spanish Mackerel 56
King Mackerel...............57
Skipjack Tuna 58
PORGIES
Scup 59
Sheepshead 60
ROCKFISH
Redfish 61
SALMON
Atlantic Salmon 62
SHARKS
Spiny Dogfish 63
Smooth Dogfish 64
Sand Shark..................65
Blue Shark 66
Sandbar Shark 67
SMELT
American Smelt 68
WOLFFISH
Atlantic Wolffish 69
WRASSES
Cunner 70
Tautog 71
PUFFER
Northern Puffer 72

SWORDFISH
Swordfish...................73
COBIA
Cobia 74
DOLPHIN
Dolphin 75
SPADEFISH
Atlantic Spadefish............76
BARRACUDA
Great Barracuda 77
BONEFISH
Bonefish....................78
CATFISHES
Sea Catfish..................79
Gafftopsail Catfish 80
GRUNTS
White Grunt 81
Pigfish 82
JACKS & POMPANO
Great Amberjack.............83
Crevalle Jack 84
Pompano 85
Glossary................. 86
Index..................... 94

Preface

From the toasty beaches of Florida to the rocky, windswept shores of Canada's Maritime Provinces, the waters of the Atlantic Ocean abound with fish in a myriad of varieties. Fishermen along this coast can take advantage of the sport—and provide tasty food for the table—any month of the year. This book, based on United States government publications, is a handy guide to the type of fish that range different parts of the coast and the best seasons for catching them. It also provides such important facts as the best bait and lures to use and the habits of the different species.

Included here are both inshore and offshore fish, big gamefish, and fish taken for the pan, as well as some that are not commonly the targets of anglers but make good fishing for people who know about them. On virtually any part of the Atlantic Coast there are fish that offer as much sport as any in the world. Among them are billfish such as marlin and swordfish, mako sharks, striped bass, and dolphin. We hope that the information in this book will encourage anglers to take advantage of the great natural and recreational resource at their doorstep.

STRIPED BASS
Morone saxatilis

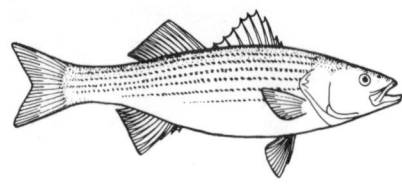

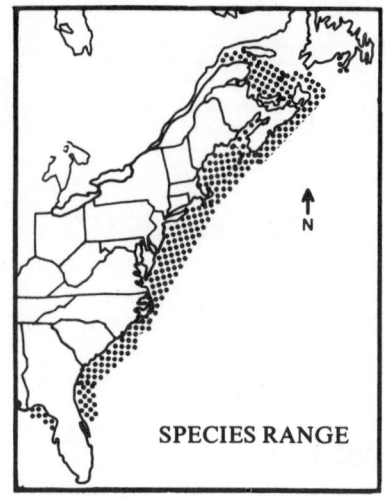

SPECIES RANGE

STRIPED BASS, *Morone saxatilis*. Rock, rockfish, striper. See white perch. SIZE: Largest recorded 125 lbs; tackle record 73 lbs; avg. 1-2 lbs; over 40 lbs unusual. HABITS: Schooling and anadromous. Occur in fresh, brackish and salt water over any type of bottom. During spring adult striped bass move towards the upper Bay and into fresh water rivers to spawn. During summer they school in lower portions of tributaries and the open Bay. During fall they usually feed along the shore and in creeks. During winter striped bass concentrate in deep portions of the Bay and lower tributaries, in depths of 20-150 ft, but are active enough to be taken by anglers in water only warmer than 39°F. SEASON: All year; best fishing mid March —May and late September—December. FISHING METHODS: Casting, bottom fishing and live lining from shore; these methods plus trolling, jigging and chumming from boats. Check state regulations on size, quantity and season. BAITS: Worms, clams, soft or shedder crab, shrimp, eels and other live baitfish. Also weighted bucktails, spoons, jigs, feathers, plugs, and imitation eels or worms.

NOTES   NOTES

DATE	LOCATION	BAIT	COMMENTS

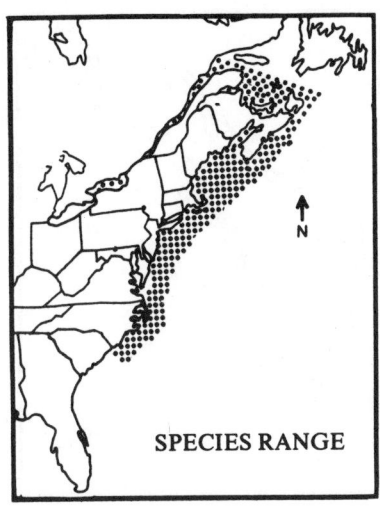

SPECIES RANGE

WHITE PERCH
Morone americanus

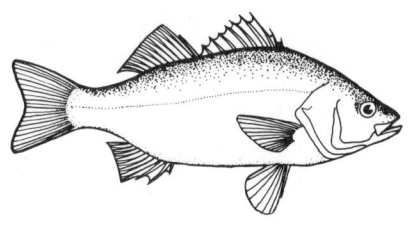

WHITE PERCH, *Morone americanus*. Perch, black perch, stiff-back perch, blue-nosed perch. See silver perch. Distinguished from striped bass by having the spiny and soft dorsal fins connected and the 2nd and 3rd anal fin spines of equal length. In the striped bass the dorsal fins are separated and the 2nd spine of the anal fin is shorter than the 3rd. SIZE: Largest recorded 4¾ lbs; avg. ⅓ - ½ lb; over 2 lbs unusual. HABITS: Resident, schooling and anadromous. Occur in fresh, brackish and salt water. During warm months most white perch occur in the lower section of tributary streams. During spring adults move upstream to spawn in fresh water; during winter they retreat downstream to deep water, some to 120 ft in channels and deep holes. SEASON: Taken all year; best fishing mid March—May and October—November. FISHING METHODS: Bottom fishing, live lining, chumming, jigging and casting from shore or boats. BAITS: Shrimp, worms, clams and small silversides or killifish; also small spoons, spinners, jigs and wet or streamer flies.

NOTES   NOTES

DATE	LOCATION	BAIT	COMMENTS

BLACK SEA BASS
Centropristis striata

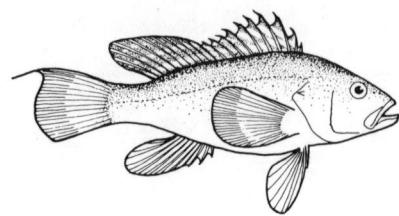
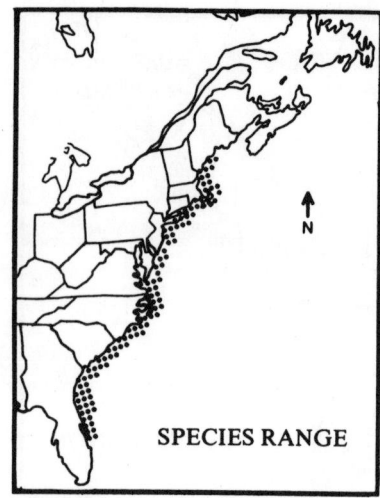

SPECIES RANGE

BLACK SEA BASS, *Centropristis striata*. Black Will, sea bass. SIZE: Largest recorded 8 lbs; tackle record 8 lbs; avg. ¼ - ⅓ lb; over ¾ lb unusual. HABITS: Gregarious and migratory. Lives on or near rock or shell bottom and around wrecks, pilings, wharfs, rock jetties or breakwaters. Black sea bass occur in the lower half of the Bay and are most common near the entrance. During warm months they occur in depths to 50 ft; during cold months they migrate out of the Bay and into deeper ocean water. SEASON: May—October. FISHING METHODS: Most caught in water warmer than 55°F from 10-30 ft deep by bottom fishing from drifting or anchored boats. A few taken from shore by bottom fishing. BAITS: Squid, clams, crabs, worms, shrimp and cut fish.

NOTES

DATE	LOCATION	BAIT	COMMENTS

ROCK SEA BASS

Centropristis philadelphica

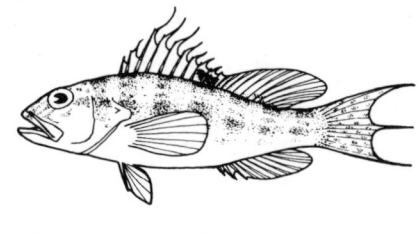

ROCK SEA BASS, *Centropristis philadelphica*. Sea bass, rock bass. Distinguished from black sea bass by having 6 or 7 broad vertical bars or stripes on back and sides, and a distinct black spot at base of last three dorsal spines. Black sea bass have no vertical bars or stripes and no large distinct spot. SIZE: To 1 lb; avg. ¼-⅓ lb; over ¾ lb unusual. Most anglers make no distinction between rock sea bass and black sea bass. HABITS, SEASON, FISHING METHODS and BAITS are the same as for black sea bass.

NOTES   NOTES

DATE	LOCATION	BAIT	COMMENTS

RED GROUPER
Epinephelus morio

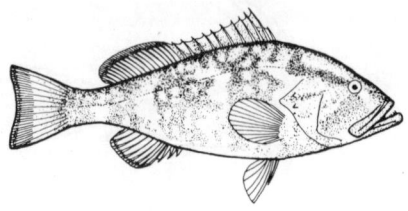

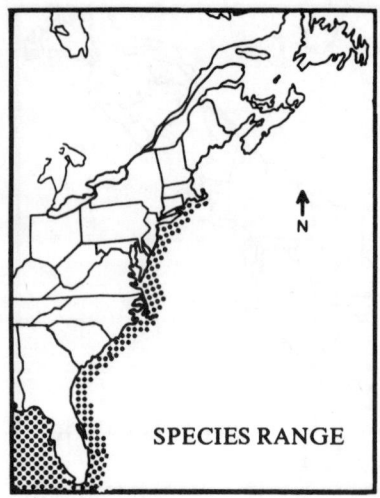

SPECIES RANGE

RED GROUPER, *Epinephelus morio*. Grouper. Distinguished from most other groupers by the edges of the membranes between the dorsal spines being slightly curved or nearly straight. In most other groupers they are deeply notched. SIZE: To 50 lbs; avg. 4-6 lbs; over 25 lbs unusual. HABITS: Occur from shore to depths of at least 900 ft, sometimes on smooth sand or mud, but most frequently around wrecks or on high relief bottom of coral and rocks encrusted with living organisms. SEASON: All year. Fishing is fairly uniform throughout the year. FISHING METHODS: Bottom fishing from anchored or drifting boats. Some caught by jigging or trolling near bottom. BAITS: Squid, shrimp, cut fish and live fish; also stripbait, weighted bucktails, jigs and feathers.

NOTES   NOTES

DATE	LOCATION	BAIT	COMMENTS

SPECIES RANGE

WARSAW GROUPER
Epinephelus nigritus

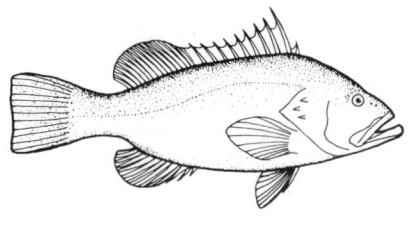

WARSAW GROUPER, *Epinephelus nigritus.* Grouper, warsaw, black jewfish, giant sea bass. Miscalled jewfish and black grouper. Distinguished from most other groupers by having 10 dorsal spines, and the edge of the tail being nearly straight. SIZE: To 500 lbs; avg. 15-25 lbs; over 150 lbs unusual. HABITS: Occur from shore to depths of 600 ft or more, especially around wrecks or on high relief bottom consisting of coral and rocks. Although usually near bottom, they may swim into mid water in pursuit of prey. SEASON: All year; best fishing November—April. FISHING METHODS: Bottom fishing, jigging or deep trolling from boats. BAITS: Squid, shrimp, crabs, spiny lobster, cut fish, whole ballyhoo, mullet or little tuna, and live pinfish or grunt; also stripbait, feather-stripbait combination, spoons, jigs and plugs.

NOTES   NOTES

DATE	LOCATION	BAIT	COMMENTS

GAG GROUPER
Mycteroperca microlepis

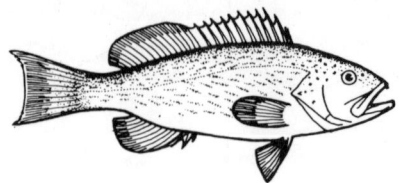

SPECIES RANGE

GAG GROUPER, *Mycteroperca microlepis*. Grouper, gray grouper. Small ones caught in shallow water are called grass grouper. Sometimes miscalled black grouper. Usually distinguished from other groupers by the more or less plain coloration and the crescent-shaped edge of the tail. SIZE: To 51 lbs; avg. 2-6 lbs; over 20 lbs unusual. HABITS: Occur to depths of 400 ft or more, especially on high relief bottom consisting of rock or coral and around wrecks. During winter and spring occur in shallow water; during summer and fall in deeper water. Small fish occur both inshore and offshore. As they grow larger, they tend to remain offshore. SEASON: All year; best fishing March—April and July—August. FISHING METHODS: Bottom fishing, live lining, jigging and casting from shore; these methods plus trolling near bottom from boats. BAITS: Shrimp, squid, cut fish, and live pinfish or grunts; also weighted bucktails, jigs, spoons and feathers.

NOTES

DATE	LOCATION	BAIT	COMMENTS

SPECKLED HIND
Epinephelus drummondhayi

SPECIES RANGE

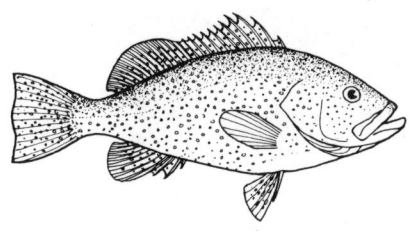

SPECKLED HIND, *Epinephelus drummondhayi*. Grouper, Kitty Mitchell. Distinguished from other groupers by being dark red or yellow-brown, densely covered with small white spots, and by the edge of the tail being nearly straight. SIZE: To 50 lbs; avg. 6-10 lbs; over 30 lbs unusual. HABITS: These bottom dwellers occur on rock or coral bottom and around wrecks to depths of 300 ft or more. SEASON: All year in depths over 120 ft; during warm months in shallower water. FISHING METHODS: Bottom fishing from anchored or drifting boats. BAITS: Cut or whole fish, squid and shrimp.

NOTES　　　　　　　　　　　　　　　　　　NOTES

DATE	LOCATION	BAIT	COMMENTS

JEWFISH

Epinephelus itajara

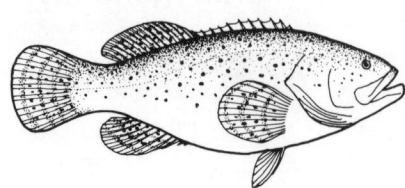

SPECIES RANGE

JEWFISH, *Epinephelus itajara*. Spotted jewfish, spotted grouper. Distinguished from other groupers by the short dorsal spines, dark spots, and rounded tail. The young have 5 dark bars on each side which disappear with age. SIZE: To over 800 lbs; tackle record 680 lbs; avg. 30-60 lbs; over 250 lbs unusual. HABITS: Although some occur in depths of 100 ft or more, most are inshore of the 70 ft bottom contour. Favor wrecks, ledges, caves, jetties, and deep holes near bridge abutments. Small ones more active than large ones. SEASON: All year. FISHING METHODS: Bottom fishing from shore or boats. Small ones take artificial lures. BAITS: Crabs, spiny lobster, live or dead fish, and clams; also jigs, plugs and feathers.

NOTES NOTES

DATE	LOCATION	BAIT	COMMENTS

BLACK GROUPER
Mycteroperca bonaci

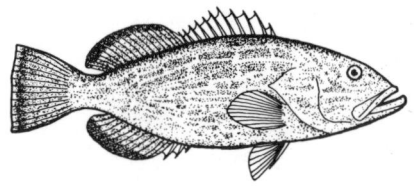

BLACK GROUPER, *Mycteroperca bonaci*. Blackfin grouper. Sometimes miscalled gag grouper. Usually distinguished from other groupers by the large, dark rectangular-shaped blotches arranged in rows on the body. SIZE: To over 100 lbs; avg. 3-7 lbs; over 30 lbs unusual. HABITS: Occur to depths of 400 ft or more on high relief bottom of coral and rocks encrusted with living organisms, or around wrecks. Small fish occur both inshore and offshore. As they grow larger, they tend to remain offshore. SEASON: All year; best fishing December—April. FISHING METHODS: Bottom fishing, live lining, jigging or trolling near bottom from boats. BAITS: Whole or cut fish, crabs, spiny lobsters, shrimp and live pinfish, grunt or snapper; also stripbait, feather-stripbait combination, spoons, plugs, jigs and weighted bucktails.

NOTES   NOTES

DATE	LOCATION	BAIT	COMMENTS

NASSAU GROUPER
Epinephelus striatus

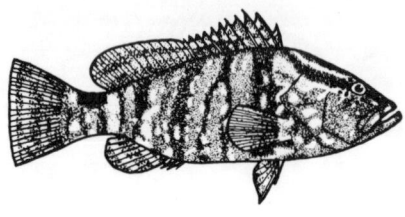

SPECIES RANGE

NASSAU GROUPER, *Epinephelus striatus*. Grouper. Distinguished from other groupers by the dark blotch on the narrow part of the tail, and the dark bars on the head and body. SIZE: To 55 lbs; avg. 2-4 lbs; over 20 lbs unusual. HABITS: Occur from the shore to depths of at least 200 ft on high relief bottom of coral and rocks or around wrecks. Small fish occur from shallow to deep water. As they grow larger, they tend to remain in deep water. SEASON: All year. FISHING METHODS: Bottom fishing from shore or boats. Small fish are caught by casting, jigging or trolling near bottom. BAITS: Cut fish, squid, shrimp, spiny lobster and live fish; also weighted bucktails and feathers.

NOTES

DATE	LOCATION	BAIT	COMMENTS

SPECIES RANGE

BLUEFISH

Pomatomus saltatrix

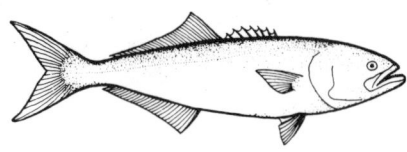

BLUEFISH, *Pomatomus saltatrix*. Blues; small fish called tailors, tailor blues or snappers. SIZE: Largest recorded 35 lbs; tackle record 31 lbs 12 oz; avg. ½-1½ lbs; over 5 lbs unusual. HABITS: Pelagic, schooling and migratory. Bluefish occur usually near the surface but sometimes throughout the water column. Numbers can fluctuate greatly from year to year. In years of abundance, bluefish occur throughout the Bay in salt and brackish water. SEASON: May—October; best fishing September—October. FISHING METHODS: Casting, bottom fishing or live lining from shore; these methods plus trolling, jigging and chumming from boats. Most bluefish are caught in water of 62° — 75°F within 45 feet of the surface. Check state regulations on size limit. BAITS: Spoons, weighted bucktails, jigs, feathers, tube lures and plugs; also worms, clams, eels and small baitfish.

NOTES   NOTES

DATE	LOCATION	BAIT	COMMENTS

ATLANTIC COD
Gadus morhua

SPECIES RANGE

ATLANTIC COD, *Gadus morhua*. Cod. See Atlantic tomcod. SIZE: Largest recorded 211½ lbs; tackle record 98¾ lbs; avg. 2-4 lbs inshore and 5-11 lbs offshore; over 50 lbs unusual. HABITS: Occur near bottom especially over ledges and slopes of shoals. Frequent rock, gravel, shell or sand bottom. During March—April on soft mud-sand. Adult cod generally occur in water colder than 50° to 55°F from near shore to 1,200 ft. SEASON: Taken all year in depths over 150 ft; November—April in shallower water. Best fishing March—April and November—December in depths of 30 to 210 ft. FISHING METHODS: Bottom fishing or jigging from boats. A few taken while casting from shore. BAITS: Sand lance, squid, crabs, clams, worms and cut fish; also jigs.

NOTES

DATE	LOCATION	BAIT	COMMENTS

POLLOCK

Pollachius virens

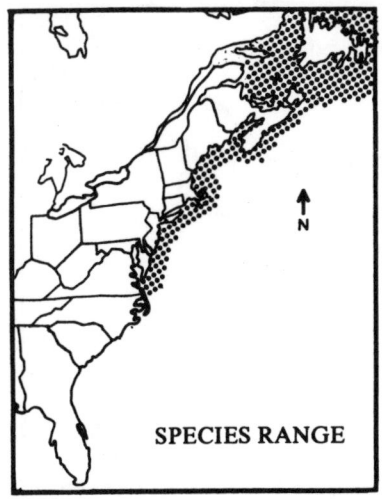

SPECIES RANGE

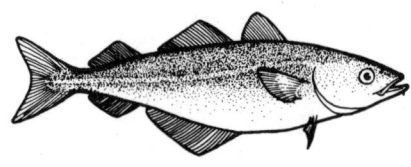

POLLOCK, *Pollachius virens*. Boston bluefish, rip pollock; fish to 5 lbs called harbor pollock; those over 5 lbs called sea pollock. Distinguished from cods by a forked tail and projecting lower jaw. SIZE: Largest recorded 70 lbs; tackle record 43 lbs; avg. 2-5 lbs; over 15 lbs unusual. HABITS: Pelagic and schooling. Occur from the surface to 600 ft in water of 31° to 60°F. SEASON: Taken in depths over 150 ft all year and in shallower water late September—early June. Best fishing mid April —early June and October—December in depths to 210 ft and water of 35° to 52°F. FISHING METHODS: Live lining, bottom fishing or casting from shore; these plus jigging and trolling from boats. BAITS: Sand lance, worms, squid, clams and cut fish. Artificial lures are best and include jigs, plastic tube lures, spoons, plugs, spinners and flies.

NOTES   NOTES

DATE	LOCATION	BAIT	COMMENTS

HADDOCK

Melanogrammus aeglefinus

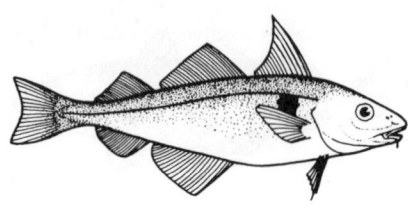

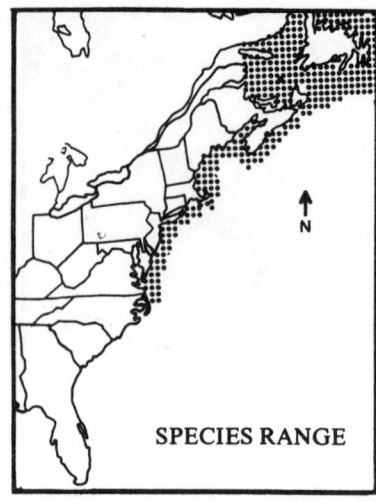

SPECIES RANGE

HADDOCK, *Melanogrammus aeglefinus.* Fish to 2½ or 3 lbs called scrod or snapper haddock. Distinguished from cods and pollock by the dusky shoulder blotch and dark lateral line. SIZE: Largest recorded 37 lbs; average 3-6 lbs; over 10 lbs unusual. HABITS: Occur on gravel, pebble, hard sand, shell or firm clay bottom. Often in gullies between ledges or rock outcrops. On soft clay or mud during April. Haddock occur in water of 34° to 60°F and to depths of 600 ft or more. More gregarious than cod, haddock travel in large aggregations near the bottom. SEASON: Taken in depths over 240 ft all year. Anglers catch most April—October in water of 45° to 52°F and depths of 90 to 250 ft. FISHING METHODS: Bottom fishing from anchored or slow-drifting boats. BAITS: Sand lance, squid, clams, mussels, worms and cut fish. Occasionally taken on small jigs.

NOTES   NOTES

DATE	LOCATION	BAIT	COMMENTS

WHITE HAKE
Urophycis tenuis

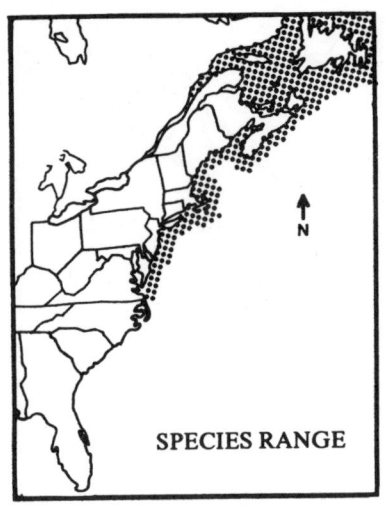

SPECIES RANGE

WHITE HAKE, *Urophycis tenuis*. Hake, miscalled silver hake. Distinguished from squirrel hake by having about 12 rows of scales between the lateral line and the base of the dorsal fin. Squirrel hake have about 9 such rows of scales. SIZE: To 48 lbs; avg. 4-9 lbs; over 20 lbs unusual. HABITS: Occur on mud or other soft bottom from the tide-line to depths over 3,000 ft. Small white hake found inshore and offshore; large fish usually in depths over 120 ft. Feed primarily at night. SEASON: Taken all year in depths over 120 ft. FISHING METHODS: Bottom fishing and jigging from shore or boats. BAITS: Clams, mussels, worms, shrimp, sand lance and cut fish. Jigs especially good for large fish.

NOTES   NOTES

DATE	LOCATION	BAIT	COMMENTS

SQUIRREL HAKE
Urophycis chuss

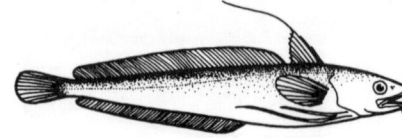
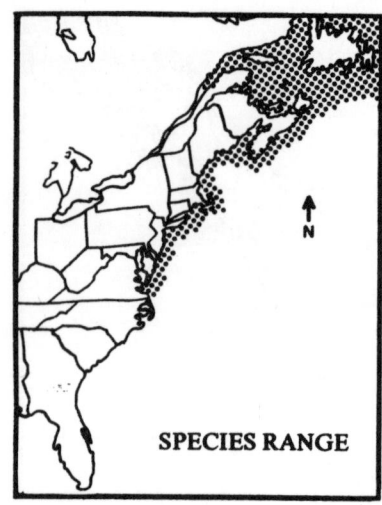

SPECIES RANGE

SQUIRREL HAKE, *Urophycis chuss.* Hake, mud hake, brown hake, ling. See white hake for distinguishing features. SIZE: To 7 lbs; average ¾-2 lbs; over 4 lbs unusual. HABITS: Occur on soft clay or mud and sand bottom. During warm months small squirrel hake are found inshore and offshore but large fish usually in depths over 90 ft. Feed primarily at night. SEASON: Taken all year in depths of 120 ft or more; best fishing March—April and October—December in depths of 10 to 180 ft. FISHING METHODS: Bottom fishing from shore; this plus jigging from boats. BAITS: Clams, worms, squid, sand lance and cut fish; also small jigs.

NOTES   NOTES

DATE	LOCATION	BAIT	COMMENTS

CUSK

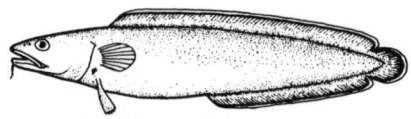

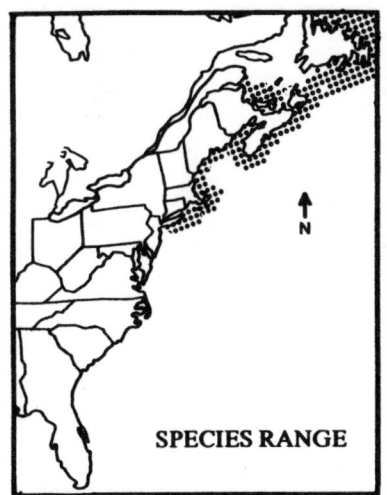

SPECIES RANGE

CUSK, *Brosme brosme*. SIZE: To 31 lbs; average 6-12 lbs; over 20 lbs unusual. HABITS: Sedentary and solitary. A bottom dweller which prefers areas with high relief such as rock out-crops. Also occur on gravel, pebble or mud bottom, but seldom on smooth, clean sand except in the Great South Channel east of Cape Cod. Occur in water of 33° to 50°F and depths to 700 ft or more. SEASON: Taken all year. Most are caught from May—October in water of 41° to 46°F and depths of 180 to 300 ft. FISHING METHODS: Bottom fishing from anchored or slow-drifting boats. BAITS: Clams, whelk, squid, crabs and cut fish. Also taken on weighted bucktails and diamond jigs.

NOTES NOTES

DATE	LOCATION	BAIT	COMMENTS

ATLANTIC TOMCOD
Microgadus tomcod

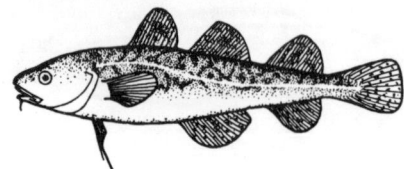
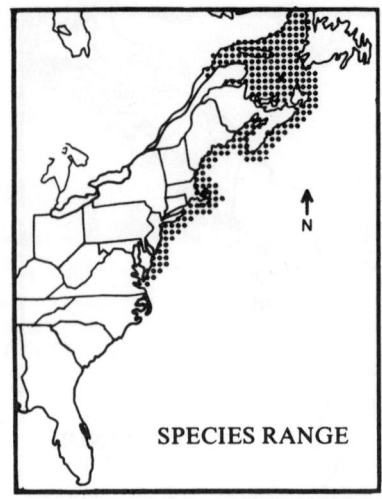

SPECIES RANGE

ATLANTIC TOMCOD, *Microgadus tomcod.* Tomcod, frostfish, tommy cod. Distinguished from cod by a rounded tail and the 2nd pelvic ray being about 1½ times the length of the next longest ray. Cod have a slightly concave tail and 2nd pelvic ray is 1¼ times the length of the next longest ray. SIZE: To 1½ lbs; avg. ¼ - ⅔ lb; over 1 lb unusual. HABITS: Usually occur in estuaries, rivers and along the coast in depths less than 36 ft. Frequent sand, mud, gravel, stone or rock bottom. Tomcod move into or towards rivers in the fall where they spawn from November through Febuary. SEASON: Taken all year; best fishing late October—December. FISHING METHODS: Bottom fishing or jigging from shore or boats. Also speared during the winter. BAITS: Worms, clams, mussels, cut fish and small jigs.

NOTES   NOTES

DATE	LOCATION	BAIT	COMMENTS

SILVER HAKE
Merluccius bilinearis

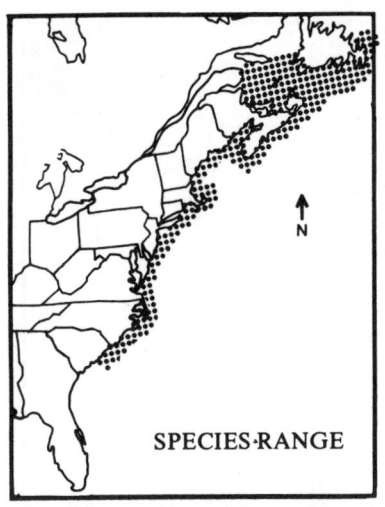

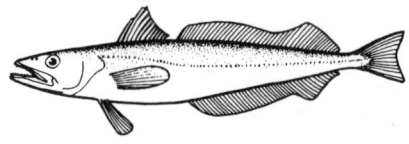

SILVER HAKE, *Merluccius bilinearis*. Whiting, frostfish. SIZE: To 5½ lbs; avg. ⅓ - ¾ lb; over 2½ lbs unusual. HABITS: Migratory and schooling. Occur from the surface at the tide-line to depths of 2,400 ft or more in water of 38° to 64°F. Usually remain close to bottom during daylight and move towards the surface or into shallow water at night. Sometimes they drive bait fish ashore and strand themselves in pursuit. SEASON: Taken in depths over 120 ft all year; in shallower water October—March. Best fishing late October—December. FISHING METHODS: Live lining, bottom fishing or casting from shore; these plus trolling, chumming or jigging from boats. Also speared at night with the aid of a light. BAITS: Clams, worms or cut fish; also jigs, spoons, spinners or plugs.

NOTES   NOTES

DATE	LOCATION	BAIT	COMMENTS

EEL

Anguilla rostrata

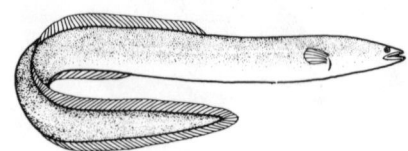

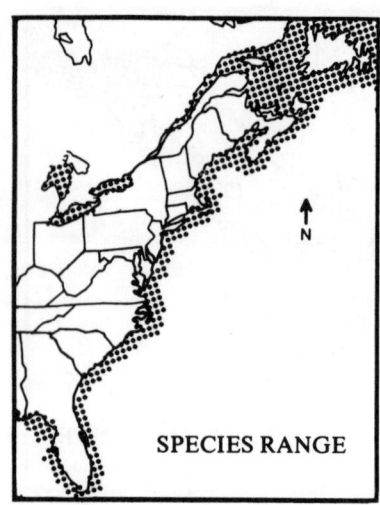

SPECIES RANGE

EEL, *Anguilla rostrata*. SIZE: Largest recorded 16 lbs; avg. ½-2 lbs; over 5 lbs unusual. HABITS: Catadromous. Young (elvers) enter estuaries in the spring. Some remain in estuaries while others migrate varying distances, sometimes hundreds of miles, up rivers and streams. Occur on any type of bottom in ponds, rivers, estuaries and near the ocean shore. Active during warm months; embedded in mud during cold months. After living in fresh or brackish water, sometimes as long as 20 years, they return to the deep ocean to spawn and subsequently die. SEASON: Late March—December; best fishing for large eels in September and October. FISHING METHODS: Bottom fishing from shore; this method plus jigging from boats. BAITS: Any natural bait; also small jigs and weighted bucktails.

NOTES   NOTES

DATE	LOCATION	BAIT	COMMENTS

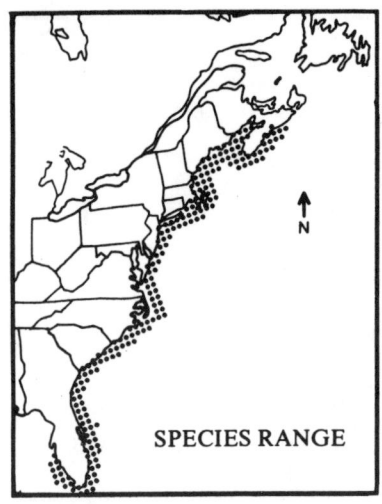

GRAY SEA TROUT
Cynoscion regalis

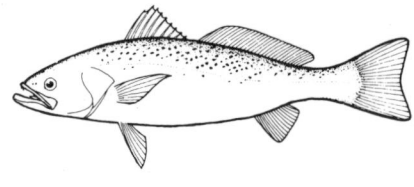

SPECIES RANGE

GRAY SEA TROUT, *Cynoscion regalis*. Trout, gray trout, sea trout, weakfish, gray weakfish. See spotted sea trout. SIZE: Largest recorded 30 lbs; tackle record 19½ lbs; avg. ¼-¾ lb; over 4 lbs unusual. HABITS: Schooling and migratory. Most abundant in the brackish water of the Bay and river mouths. They are found over any type of bottom, but favor sandy areas, especially with eel grass beds. SEASON: May or June—October or mid November; best fishing in September and October. Most are caught a few feet off the bottom in depths of 6 to 45 ft. FISHING METHODS: Bottom fishing, live lining, casting, chumming and jigging from shore; these methods plus trolling from boats. Check state regulations on size limits. BAITS: Shrimp, squid, silversides, mullet, soft or shedder crab, worms, clams, mussels, cut fish and live killifish. Also spinners, spoons, plugs, jigs and weighted bucktails.

NOTES

DATE	LOCATION	BAIT	COMMENTS

NORTHERN KINGFISH
Menticirrhus saxatilis

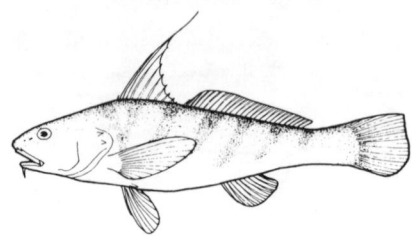

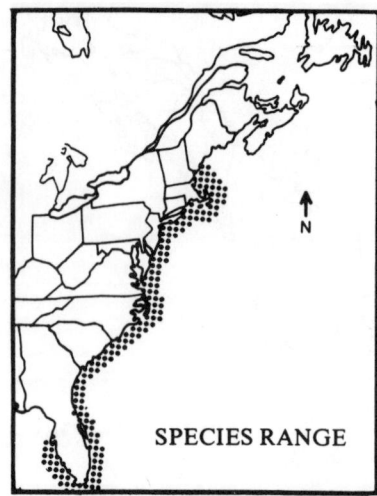

SPECIES RANGE

NORTHERN KINGFISH, *Menticirrhus saxatilis*. Kingfish, roundhead, whiting, king whiting. Miscalled mullet and sea mullet. See southern kingfish. SIZE: To 3⅓ lbs; avg. ⅓-⅔ lb; over 2 lbs unusual. HABITS: An inshore fish occurring from the tide-line to depths of 45 ft in salt and brackish water warmer than 46°-50°F. Aggregate on sand, shell or gravel bottom, especially near sand bars or along the edges of channels. SEASON: Late April or May—mid November; best fishing August—October. FISHING METHODS: Bottom fishing from shore; this method plus chumming from anchored or drifting boats. BAITS: Worms, squid, clams, mussels, shrimp, silversides, soft or shedder crab and cut fish.

NOTES

DATE	LOCATION	BAIT	COMMENTS

SPOT

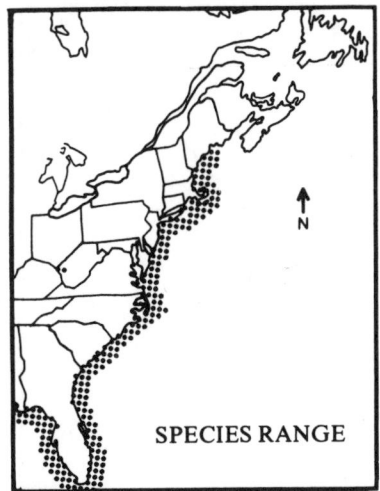

Leiostomus xanthurus

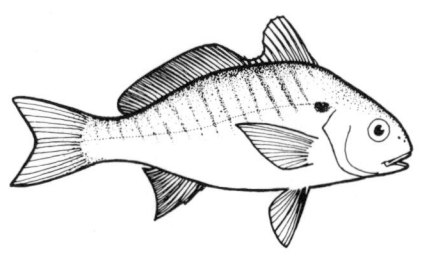

SPOT, *Leiostomus xanthurus*. Norfolk spot, Ocean View spot, Layafette. Distinguished from silver perch by having a dark shoulder spot and a slightly forked tail. In contrast, silver perch have no spot and their tails are nearly square. SIZE: To 2¼ lbs; avg. ¼-½ lb; over 1 lb unusual. HABITS: Most occur in salt and brackish water, a few in fresh water. These bottom feeders usually aggregate according to size, and frequent sand or mud bottom and shellfish beds. Adults are migratory; young fish may remain in the Bay all year, many in deep holes or channels during winter. SEASON: May or June—October or early November; best fishing mid August—early October. FISHING METHODS: Bottom fishing from shore; this method plus chumming from boats. BAITS: Worms, shrimp, soft crab, clams and cut fish.

NOTES | NOTES

DATE	LOCATION	BAIT	COMMENTS

SILVER PERCH
Bairdiella chrysura

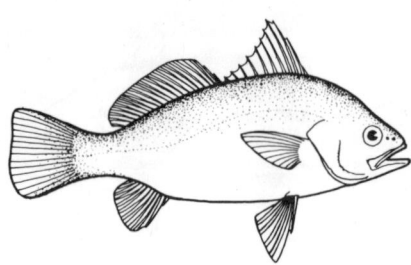

SPECIES RANGE

SILVER PERCH, *Bairdiella chrysura*. Sand perch, white sand perch, yellowtail, King William. Often miscalled white perch. See spot. Distinguished from white perch by having 2 anal fin spines and the lateral line extending onto tail. White perch have 3 anal fin spines and lateral line does not extend onto tail. SIZE: to ¾ lb; avg. ¼ – ⅓ lb; over ½ lb unusual. HABITS: Occur in salt and brackish water on sand, mud or shell bottom; especially sandy-mud with eel grass. Adults are migratory; young fish remain year-round in the Bay. SEASON: April—October or mid November; best fishing in September and early October. FISHING METHODS: Bottom fishing from shore, this method plus live lining and chumming from boats. Usually taken as an incidental fish. BAITS: Worms, shrimp, clams, mussels, soft crab and cut fish; also small weighted bucktails.

NOTES | NOTES

DATE	LOCATION	BAIT	COMMENTS

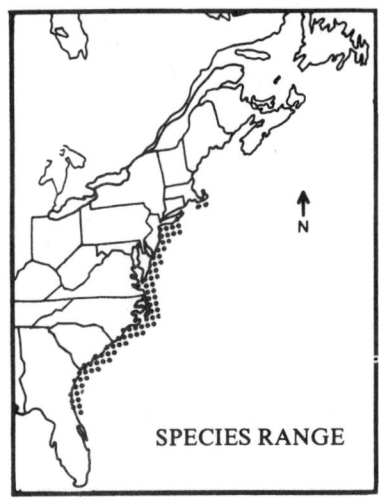

SPOTTED SEA TROUT
Cynoscion nebulosus

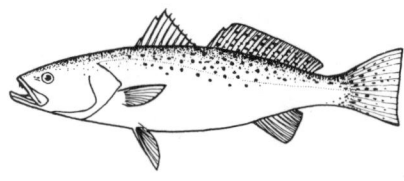

SPOTTED SEA TROUT, *Cynoscion nebulosus*. Speckled trout, trout, salmon trout. Distinguished from gray sea trout by round dark spots on upper half of body as well as on 2nd dorsal fin and tail. Gray sea trout have dark blotches, generally arranged in rows along the back, but without spots on 2nd dorsal fin and tail. SIZE: Largest recorded 16½ lbs; tackle record 15 lbs 3 oz; avg. ¾-1½ lbs; over 4 lbs unusual. HABITS: Schooling and migratory. Occur in salt and brackish water warmer than 50°-54°F, particularly the shallow water of estuaries. Found over any type of bottom but favor areas which abound with eel or other sea grass beds. SEASON: Mid May or June—early December; best fishing late July—early November. FISHING METHODS: Casting, jigging, chumming, and live lining from shore; these methods plus trolling from boats. BAITS: Plugs, weighted bucktails, jigs and spoons; also shrimp, silversides, mullet, killifish and soft or shedder crab.

NOTES   NOTES

DATE	LOCATION	BAIT	COMMENTS

RED DRUM

Sciaenops ocellata

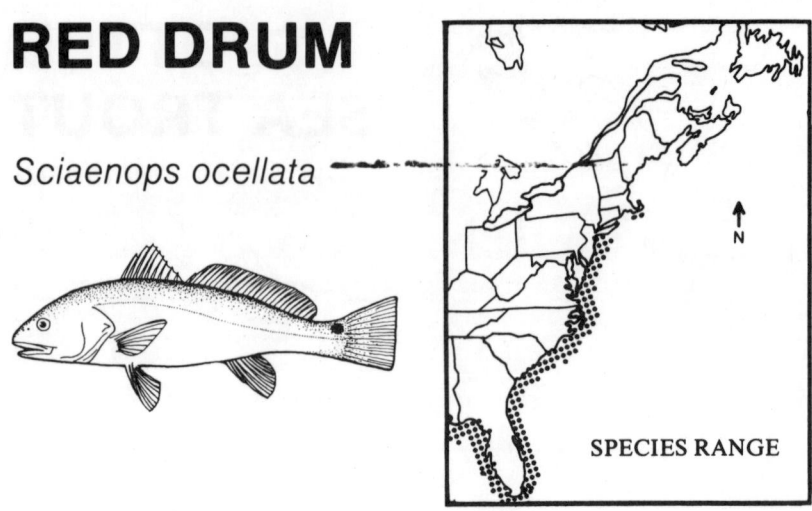

SPECIES RANGE

RED DRUM, *Sciaenops ocellata*. Channel bass; small ones sometimes called puppy drum. SIZE: Largest recorded 90 lbs; tackle record 90 lbs; small fish average 1-2 lbs and large fish 20-30 lbs; over 55 lbs unusual. HABITS: Migratory and schooling. During spring migrations, schools occur in the open Bay away from shore; during summer and fall they usually occur close to shore. SEASON: Late April or May—November; best fishing for large fish mid May—mid June, for small fish August—October. FISHING METHODS: Most are caught by bottom fishing, casting and trolling from boats; some by bottom fishing and casting from shore. BAITS: Soft or shedder crab, shrimp, clams, squid and cut mullet, spot or menhaden; also spoons, jigs and weighted bucktails.

NOTES   NOTES

DATE	LOCATION	BAIT	COMMENTS

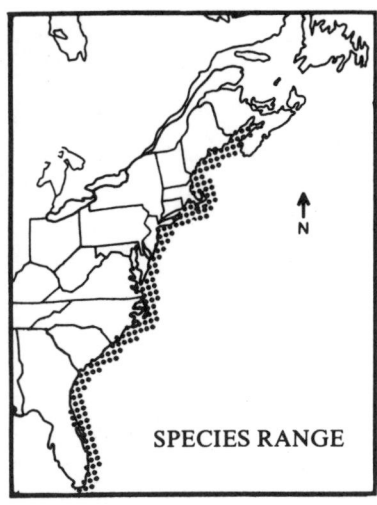

SPECIES RANGE

BLACK DRUM
Pogonias cromis

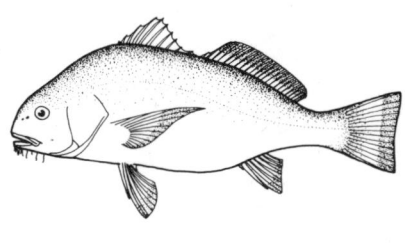

BLACK DRUM, *Pogonias cromis*. Drum; fish less than 8 lbs called puppy drum. The young are characterized by 4 to 6 broad, black bars on their sides. SIZE: Largest recorded 146 lbs; tackle record 111 lbs; puppy drum average ¾-2 lbs; and large fish 25-35 lbs; over 80 lbs unusual. HABITS: Migratory. In large aggregations during the spring migrations but usually solitary during fall. These bottom feeders occur on any type of bottom but prefer mussel, clam or oyster beds. Often around breakwaters, jetties, pilings, bridge abutments and piers. SEASON: April—October or mid November; best fishing for large fish in May and June, for small fish in September and October. FISHING METHODS: Bottom fishing, live lining or chumming from shore or boats. Casting or trolling is also effective for small fish but large fish do not ordinarily take a fast moving bait. BAITS: Clam, soft or shedder crab, shrimp and cut fish; also spoons, jigs and weighted bucktails.

NOTES   NOTES

DATE	LOCATION	BAIT	COMMENTS

ATLANTIC CROAKER
Micropogon undulatus

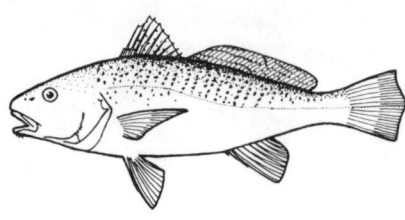

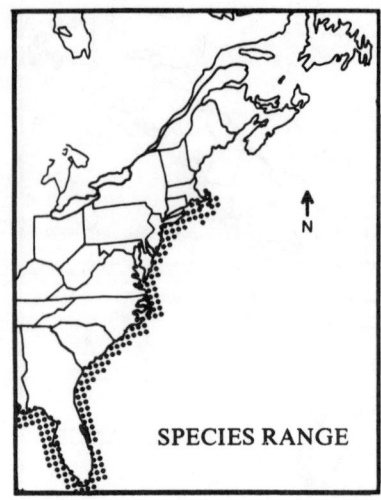

SPECIES RANGE

ATLANTIC CROAKER, *Micropogon undulatus.* Croaker, hardhead. SIZE: To 5 lbs; avg. ½-¾ lb; over 3 lbs unusual. HABITS: Migratory. A few occur in nearly fresh water, but most in salt and brackish water from a few feet below the tide-line to depths of 45 ft. This bottom feeder occurs on mud, sand, gravel or rock bottom and around shellfish beds, rock piles and wrecks. SEASON: Mid April or May—late September or October; best fishing June—early July. FISHING METHODS: Bottom fishing, jigging and chumming from anchored or drifting boats. Some caught by bottom fishing from shore. Check state regulations on size limit. BAITS: Shrimp, soft or shedder crab, clams and cut fish; also small jigs and weighted bucktails.

NOTES   NOTES

DATE	LOCATION	BAIT	COMMENTS

SOUTHERN KINGFISH
Menticirrhus americanus

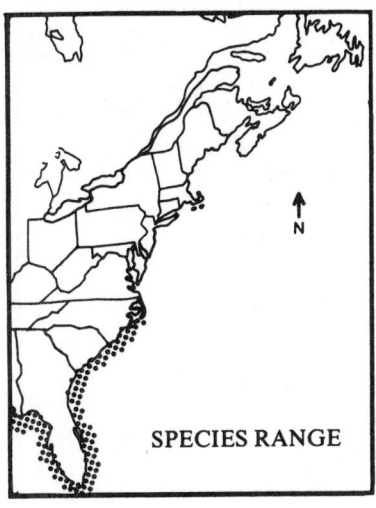

SPECIES RANGE

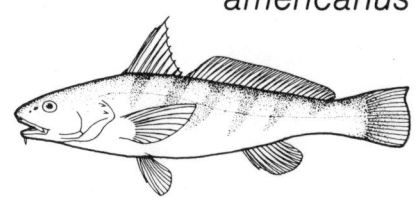

SOUTHERN KINGFISH, *Menticirrhus americanus*. Kingfish, roundhead, whiting, king whiting. Miscalled mullet and sea mullet. Distinguished from northern kingfish by having 7, rarely 8, soft anal rays; the longest spine of the 1st dorsal fin in an adult fish extends to just beyond origin of 2nd dorsal fin, and the obscure, oblique bars along the side do not form a V just behind the head. In contrast, northern kingfish usually have 8, sometimes 9, soft anal rays; the longest spine of the 1st dorsal fin in an adult extends far beyond origin of 2nd dorsal fin, and the dark, oblique bars along the side form a V just behind the head. SIZE: To 3 lbs; avg. ⅓—⅔ lb; over 1¾ lbs unusual. Northern and southern kingfish are so similar that they are considered the same species by most anglers. HABITS, SEASON, FISHING METHODS and BAITS are the same as for northern kingfish.

NOTES   NOTES

DATE	LOCATION	BAIT	COMMENTS

SILVER SEA TROUT
Cynoscion nothus

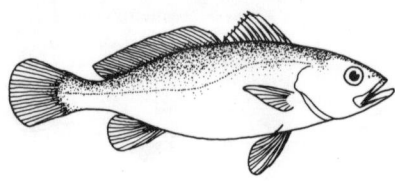
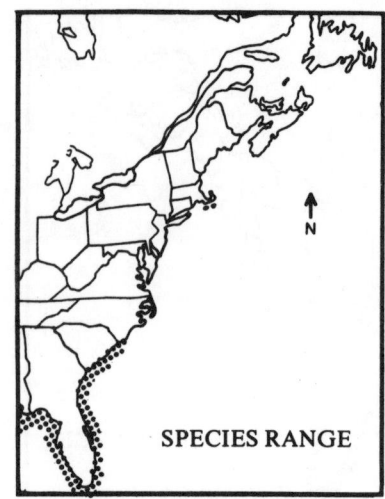

SPECIES RANGE

SILVER SEA TROUT, *Cynoscion nothus.* Trout, white trout. Distinguished from gray sea trout by having a rounded tail and usually 9, but sometimes 8 or 10, anal fin rays. Gray sea trout have slightly forked tails and 11 or 12 anal fin rays. Differs from spotted sea trout in having no round, dark spots on the upper half of the body or on the 2nd dorsal fin and tail. Spotted sea trout have these spots. SIZE: To 2 lbs; avg. ⅓ — ⅔ lb; over 1½ lbs unusual. HABITS: Occur in salt and brackish water over any type of bottom to depths of 60 ft. Otherwise, the habits of silver sea trout are similar to those of gray sea trout. SEASON: All year; best fishing March—May. FISHING METHODS: Bottom fishing, jigging, live lining and chumming from shore; these methods plus trolling from boats. Check state regulation on size limit. BAITS: Shrimp, squid, clams and cut fish; also small weighted bucktails, feathers, jigs and streamer flies.

NOTES   NOTES

DATE	LOCATION	BAIT	COMMENTS

SPECIES RANGE

GULF KINGFISH
Menticirrhus littoralis

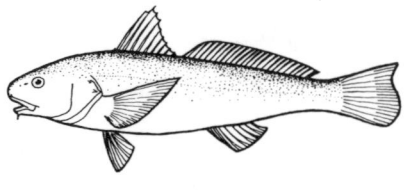

GULF KINGFISH, *Menticirrhus littoralis.* Whiting, king whiting, beach whiting, silver whiting. Distinguished from southern kingfish by the absence of dark markings on its silvery body, and by its pale gill cavity. In contrast, southern kingfish have dusky bars on back and sides, and a dark gill cavity. SIZE: To 3½ lbs; avg. ⅓ – 1 lb; over 2 lbs unusual. HABITS: Gulf kingfish prefer saltier water than southern kingfish. Although a few occur within estuaries, most remain along sandy beaches of the open ocean and near the outside mouths of inlets. SEASON, FISHING METHODS and BAITS are the same as for southern kingfish.

NOTES

DATE	LOCATION	BAIT	COMMENTS

WHITE MARLIN
Tetrapturus albidus

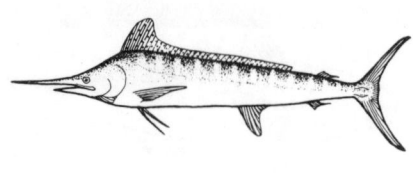

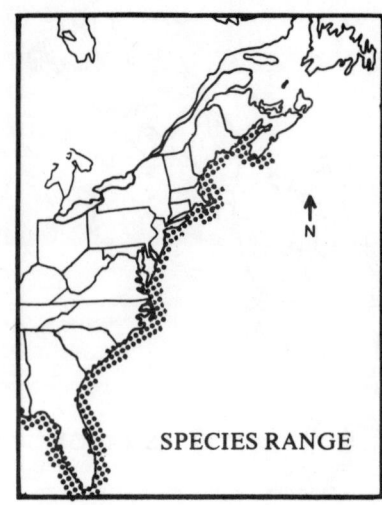

SPECIES RANGE

WHITE MARLIN, *Tetrapturus albidus*. See blue marlin. SIZE: Maximum size unrecorded; tackle record 161 lbs; avg. 50-60 lbs; over 90 lbs unusual. HABITS: Pelagic and migratory. Occur in oceanic and continental-shelf water but some come close to shore in depths as shallow as 60 ft. Travel in small groups or singly. SEASON: All year; best fishing late February or March—May or June. Most are caught near the surface in water warmer than 70°F between the 100-600 ft bottom contours. FISHING METHODS: Trolling and live lining from boats. BAITS: Stripbait, feather-stripbait or skirt-stripbait combination, and whole rigged squid, ballyhoo, mullet, Spanish mackerel or bonefish; also live bait. Some are caught on feathers, skirts, rubber squid and plugs.

NOTES   NOTES

DATE	LOCATION	BAIT	COMMENTS

SPECIES RANGE

BLUE MARLIN
Makaira nigricans

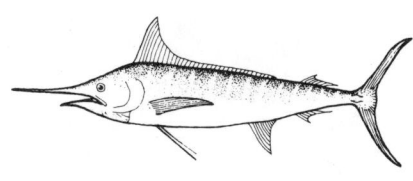

BLUE MARLIN, *Makaira nigricans*. Distinguished from white marlin by having the tips of the dorsal and anal fins pointed, and, except for very small fish, the lateral line is inconspicuous. White marlin have rounded dorsal and anal fin tips and the lateral line is conspicuous. SIZE: To over 1,700 lbs in the Atlantic Ocean; Atlantic tackle record 1,142 lbs (Pacific tackle record 1,153 lbs but fish over 2,000 lbs are reported); avg. 200-300 lbs; over 400 lbs unusual. HABITS: Pelagic and migratory. Occur in oceanic and continental-shelf water from the surface to depths of at least 300 ft. Travel in small groups or singly. SEASON: All year; best fishing January—May or June. Most are taken near the surface between the 300 and 600 ft bottom contours. FISHING METHODS: Trolling, live lining and kite fishing from boats. BAITS: Whole rigged squid, Spanish mackerel, mullet, ballyhoo, bonefish, ladyfish and little tuna; also live fish, stripbait and feather-stripbait combination.

NOTES   NOTES

DATE	LOCATION	BAIT	COMMENTS

ATLANTIC SAILFISH
Istiophorus platypterus

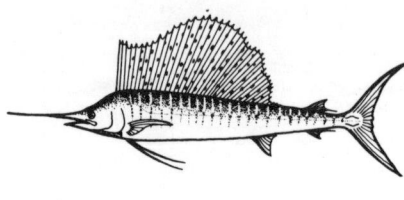

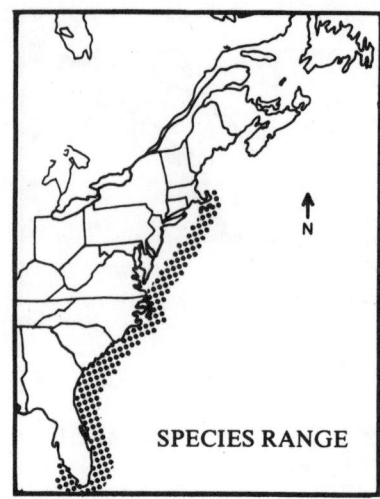

SPECIES RANGE

ATLANTIC SAILFISH, *Istiophorus platypterus.* Sailfish. SIZE: Maximum size unrecorded; Atlantic tackle record 128 lbs (Pacific tackle record 221 lbs); avg. 30-40 lbs; over 70 lbs unusual. HABITS: Pelagic and migratory. Occur in continental-shelf water usually in depths over 40 ft, but they occasionally venture close enough to shore to be caught from ocean piers. Travel in small groups or singly. Sailfish usually feed more in midwater and near bottom than at the surface. SEASON: All year; best fishing mid-October or November—April. FISHING METHODS: Trolling, live lining and kite fishing from boats. A few are caught from shore. Check state regulation on daily catch limit. BAITS: Stripbait, feather-stripbait or skirt-stripbait combination, whole rigged ballyhoo or mullet, and live blue runner, mullet, goggle-eyed scad, false pilchard, pinfish or bonefish. Some are caught on feathers, spoons, skirts and plugs.

NOTES   NOTES

DATE	LOCATION	BAIT	COMMENTS

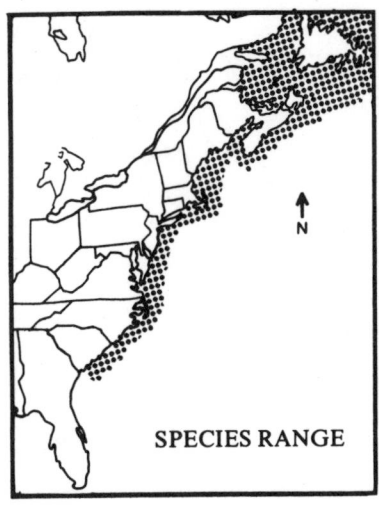

SPECIES RANGE

WINTER FLOUNDER
Pseudopleuronectes americanus

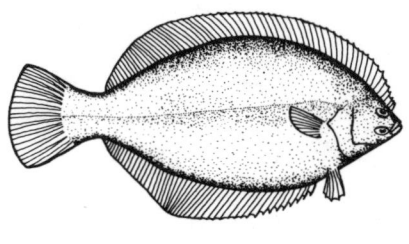

WINTER FLOUNDER, *Pseudopleuronectes americanus.* Flounder. Mis-called halibut and halibut flounder; many anglers mistake winter flounder for young summer flounder. SIZE: To 8 lbs; avg. $\frac{1}{3} - \frac{2}{3}$ lb; over 2 lbs unusual. HABITS: Year-round bottom residents on mud, sand, shell or gravel bottom; especially mud-sand around eel grass. A few ascend streams to fresh water, but most occur in salt and brackish water from the tide-line to depths of 175 ft. Small fish usually live close to shore and large fish away from shore. SEASON: Most are caught from September—May; a few the year round. Best fishing March—April and October—December. FISHING METHODS: Bottom fishing and chumming from shore and boats. BAITS: Worms, shrimp, clams, mussels, squid and cut fish.

NOTES   NOTES

DATE	LOCATION	BAIT	COMMENTS

SMOOTH FLOUNDER
Liopsetta putnami

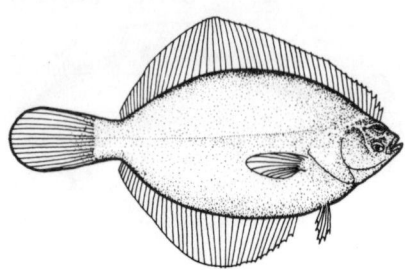

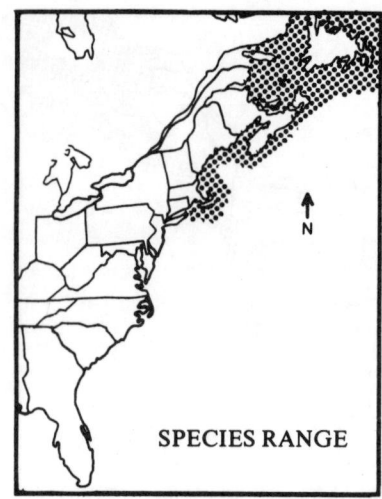

SPECIES RANGE

SMOOTH FLOUNDER, *Liopsetta putnami*. Flounder. Distinguished from winter flounder by a smooth scaleless space between the eyes and 35 to 41 anal fin rays. Winter flounder have scales between the eyes and 44 to 58 anal fin rays. SIZE: To 1½ lbs; average ⅓ - ⅔ lb; over 1 lb unusual. HABITS: Coastal bottom dweller. Occur chiefly in estuaries and sheltered bays from the tide-line to 90 ft or more in water of 30° to 60°F. Smooth flounder frequent soft mud or clay bottom and muddy-sand around eel grass. SEASON: Taken all year east of Casco Bay; best fishing June—September. From Casco Bay to Boston taken September—February; best fishing may be at any time during this period. Most are caught in depths of 10 to 30 ft. FISHING METHODS: Bottom fishing from shore and anchored or drifting boats. BAITS: Worms, squid, clams, mussels, shrimp and cut fish.

NOTES   NOTES

DATE	LOCATION	BAIT	COMMENTS

SPECIES RANGE

ATLANTIC HALIBUT
Hippoglossus hippoglossus

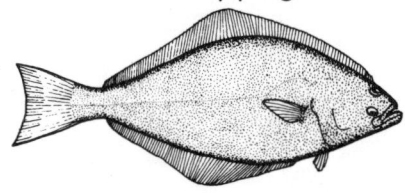

ATLANTIC HALIBUT, *Hippoglossus hippoglossus*. Halibut, fish 50 lbs or less called chicken halibut. SIZE: Largest recorded 735 lbs; avg. 30-85 lbs; over 200 lbs unusual. HABITS: Occur on sand, gravel and clay bottom but prefer sand-gravel or mud-gravel between rock outcrops and ledges. In gullies on gritty clay or clay-sand during March and April. Halibut usually feed near bottom but may pursue prey to the surface. Some are caught while attempting to steal a hooked cod, pollock or haddock. Occur in water of 34° to 59°F and depths to 3,000 ft or more. SEASON: Can be taken in depths over 300 ft all year. Anglers catch most from late March—early November in water of 37° to 48°F and depths of 90 to 270 ft. FISHING METHODS: Bottom and live-bait fishing or jigging from boats. BAITS: Live or cut fish, clams, crabs, squid, and diamond jigs.

NOTES   NOTES

DATE	LOCATION	BAIT	COMMENTS

NORTHERN FLUKE
Paralichthys dentatus

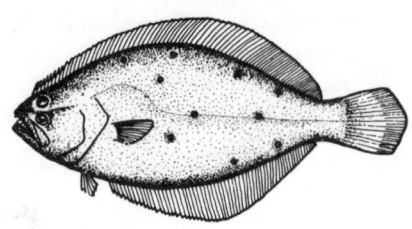

SPECIES RANGE

NORTHERN FLUKE, *Paralichthys dentatus*. Fluke, summer flounder; Large fish called doormats. See windowpane flounder. SIZE: Largest recorded 30 lbs; tackle record 20½ lbs; avg. 1-3½ lbs; over 8 lbs unusual. HABITS: Most occur in salt and brackish water; a few small ones in fresh water. Frequent gravel, sand, clay or mud bottom and around wrecks to depths of 500 ft or more. An active feeder often pursuing bait-fish to the surface. SEASON: June—mid October; best fishing July—mid September. Most caught in water 10 to 60 ft deep and warmer than 61°F. FISHING METHODS: Bottom fishing from boats and casting or bottom fishing from shore. BAITS: Smelt, squid, shrimp, clams, worms, cut fish, silversides and live killifish; also spinners and weighted bucktails.

NOTES   NOTES

DATE	LOCATION	BAIT	COMMENTS

WINDOW-PANE

Scophthalmus aquosus

SPECIES RANGE

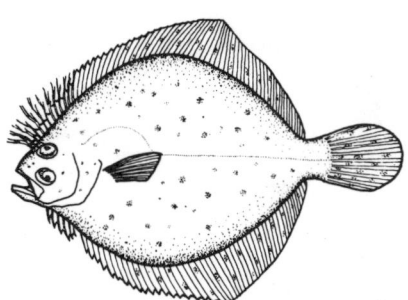

WINDOWPANE, *Scophthalmus aquosus*. Flounder, sand flounder, sand dab, sundial, see-through flounder. Distinguished from the summer flounder by the first 10-12 dorsal fin rays forming a fringed crest. Summer flounder have no fringed crest. SIZE: To 2 lbs; avg. ⅓ - ⅔ lb; over 1¼ lbs unusual. HABITS: A year-round resident in salt or brackish water. Windowpanes frequent sand, sand-mud, sand-shell, gravel and soft mud or clay bottom. Most occur in depths less than 100 ft but a few are found to 200 ft. SEASON: Taken all year; best fishing May—November. FISHING METHODS: Bottom fishing from shore and anchored or drifting boats. BAITS: Shrimp, worms, squid, clams, mussels, silversides and killifish; also weighted bucktails and jigs.

NOTES   NOTES

DATE	LOCATION	BAIT	COMMENTS

SOUTHERN FLUKE
Paralichthys lethostigma

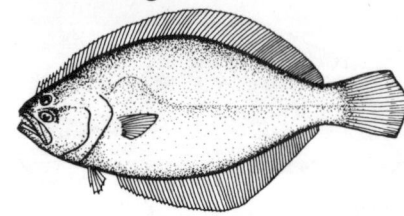

SPECIES RANGE

SOUTHERN FLUKE, *Paralichthys lethostigma*. Flounder, southern flounder. SIZE: To over 13 lbs; avg. 1-2 lbs; over 10 lbs unusual. HABITS: These bottom feeders live on mud, sand and sand-shell bottom. They occur in salt and brackish water and often ascend fresh water streams or rivers for a considerable distance. During warm months many occur near the shore in shallow estuaries; during cold months they move into deeper water. Usually feed near bottom but will pursue prey to the surface. SEASON: All year; best fishing June—November. Night spearing on shallow flats is best June—September. FISHING METHODS: Bottom fishing from shore; this method plus chumming, live lining and trolling near bottom from boats. Night spearing, called gigging or floundering, is commonly done either while wading or from boats. Check state regulation on size limit. BAITS: Killifish, squid, mullet, clams, worms and cut fish. A few are caught on jigs, spinners, spoons and weighted bucktails.

NOTES   NOTES

DATE	LOCATION	BAIT	COMMENTS

AMERICAN SHAD
Alosa sapidissima

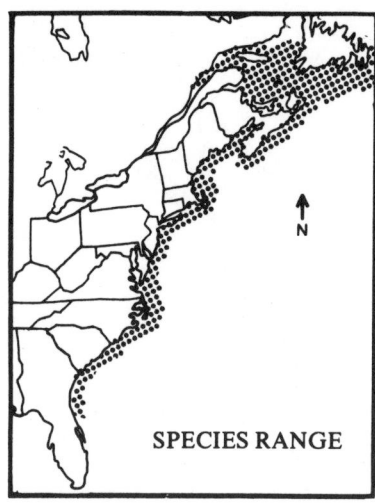

SPECIES RANGE

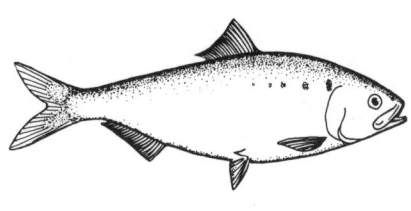

AMERICAN SHAD, *Alosa sapidissima*. Shad, white shad. Adult females are called roe or roe shad; adult males are called bucks or buck shad. SIZE: Largest recorded 14 lbs; males average 2-3½ lbs and females 3-4½ lbs; over 6 lbs unusual. See hickory shad. HABITS: Pelagic, schooling, migratory, anadromous. Although shad spend most of their lives in the ocean, adults ascend to fresh water in the spring to spawn when river temperatures reach 55°F. During the spawning run they take little or no food but will strike some artificial lures. Spawning over, spent fish return to the ocean. SEASON: March—June or July; best fishing late April—early June. FISHING METHODS: Casting from shore; this method plus trolling and jigging from boats. Angling is usually confined to the fresh water portion of tidal rivers. BAITS: Spoons, spinners, jigs, weighted bucktails and shad darts.

NOTES | NOTES

DATE	LOCATION	BAIT	COMMENTS

HICKORY SHAD
Alosa mediocris

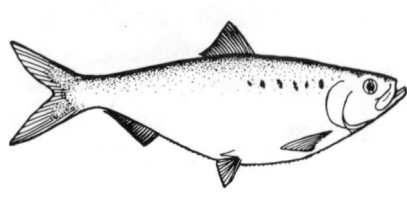

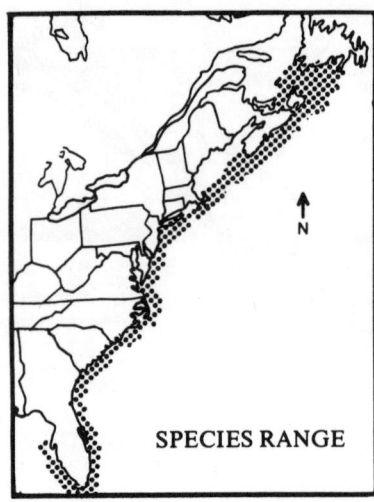

SPECIES RANGE

HICKORY SHAD, *Alosa mediocris*. Shad, hicks. Adult females are called roes; adult males are called bucks. Distinguished from American shad and other herring by the tip of the lower jaw extending noticeably beyond the upper when mouth is closed. SIZE: To 4½ lbs; avg. 1½-2½ lbs; over 3¾ lbs unusual. HABITS: Pelagic, schooling, migratory, anadromous. Occur in salt, brackish and fresh water. The spring spawning run of hickory shad into fresh water usually precedes the run of American shad by a few weeks. SEASON: Late February—November; best fishing late March—early May. A small run usually occurs late August—early October. FISHING METHODS: Casting from shore; this method plus trolling and jigging from boats. Most are caught incidentally with American shad. BAITS: Spoons, spinners, plugs, weighted bucktails and shad darts.

NOTES   NOTES

DATE	LOCATION	BAIT	COMMENTS

ATLANTIC MACKEREL
Scomber scombrus

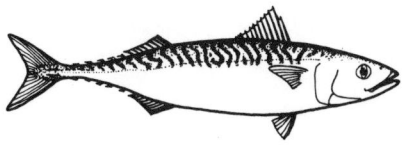

ATLANTIC MACKEREL, *Scomber scombrus*. Mackerel. Fish to 8 inches called spikes; 8-13 inch (1 lb) fish called tinkers; 1-2 lbs fish called mackerel; those above 2 lbs miscalled king mackerel. See Chub mackerel. SIZE: To 7½ lbs; avg. ½-1¼ lbs; over 2½ lbs unusual. HABITS: Pelagic, schooling, migratory. Found both offshore and inshore often entering estuaries. Occur in water of 45° to 68°F from the surface to depths of 600 ft. SEASON: Late May—mid December; best fishing September—mid November. Anglers catch most within 60 ft of the surface. FISHING METHODS: Casting or live lining from shore; these plus trolling, jigging or chumming from boats. BAITS: Sand lance, worms, clams, shrimp, squid and cut fish; also spoons, spinners, weighted bucktails, flies, jigs, and plastic tube lures.

NOTES   NOTES

DATE	LOCATION	BAIT	COMMENTS

CHUB MACKEREL
Scomber colias

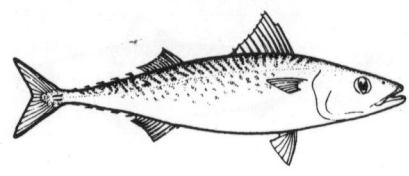

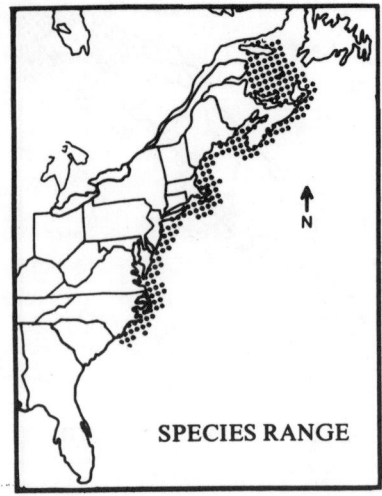

SPECIES RANGE

CHUB MACKEREL, *Scomber colias*. Mackerel, thimble-eyed mackerel. Distinguished from Atlantic mackerel by having 9-10 dorsal spines, head length going into standard body length 3-3½ times and by the silvery sides below mid-line being mottled with dusky bloches. In contrast the Atlantic mackerel has 11-14, rarely 10, dorsal spines; head length goes into standard body length 3½-4½ times and the sides below mid-line are without dusky blotches. SIZE: To 1½ lbs; avg. ⅓ - ⅔ lb; over 1 lb unusual. Although smaller in size and preferring warmer water, chub mackerel are quite similar in most respects to Atlantic mackerel. Most fishermen make no distinction between these two fish. HABITS, SEASON, FISHING METHODS and BAITS are the same as for Atlantic mackerel.

NOTES   NOTES

DATE	LOCATION	BAIT	COMMENTS

SPECIES RANGE

BLUEFIN TUNA
Thunnus thynnus

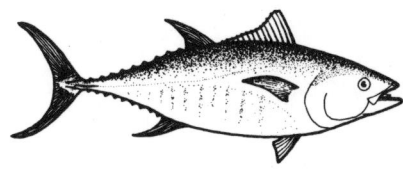

BLUEFIN TUNA, *Thunnus thynnus*. Tuna; fish to 100 lbs called school tuna, those over 100 lbs called giant tuna. SIZE: Largest recorded 1,500 lbs; tackle record 977 lbs; school tuna avg. 15-35 lbs and giant tuna 250-450 lbs; over 700 lbs unusual. HABITS: Pelagic, schooling, migratory. Range from far out at sea to close inshore, but almost always in depths of 20 ft or more. When offshore, tuna are usually found from the surface to 300 ft. Large fish occur in water warmer than 44°F, most in 54° to 67°F; small fish occur in water warmer than 60°F. SEASON: Although tuna occur from late June—early December, they are caught by anglers only from late August or September—late October. Best fishing in September. FISHING METHODS and BAITS: Fast trolling whole bait or artificial lures such as feathers and spoons for school tuna; chumming at anchor for giant tuna.

NOTES   NOTES

DATE	LOCATION	BAIT	COMMENTS

ATLANTIC BONITO
Sarda sarda

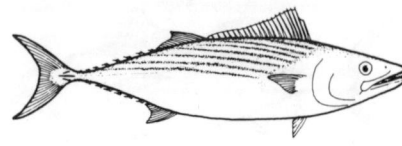

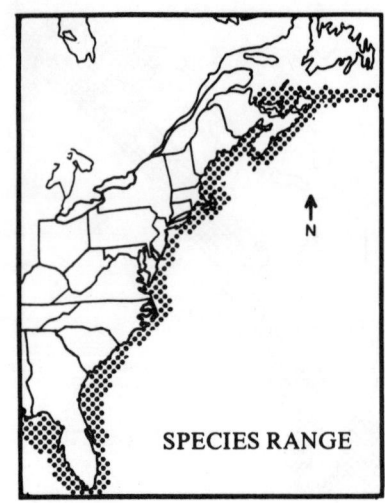

SPECIES RANGE

ATLANTIC BONITO, *Sarda sarda*. Bonito. SIZE: To 15 lbs; avg. 2-4 lbs; over 7 lbs unusual. HABITS: Pelagic, schooling and migratory. Rapid swimmers which feed mainly at or near the surface; they often jump clear of the water when in pursuit of prey. Abundance fluctuates greatly. SEASON: Late May or June—October; best fishing in August and September. FISHING METHODS: Caught by trolling at or near the surface in water warmer than 65°F; some by casting, jigging or chumming from boats. Usually caught incidentally with other pelagic fishes. BAITS: Feathers, spoons, plugs, jigs, stripbait, feather-stripbait or skirt-stripbait combination and cut fish.

NOTES   NOTES

DATE	LOCATION	BAIT	COMMENTS

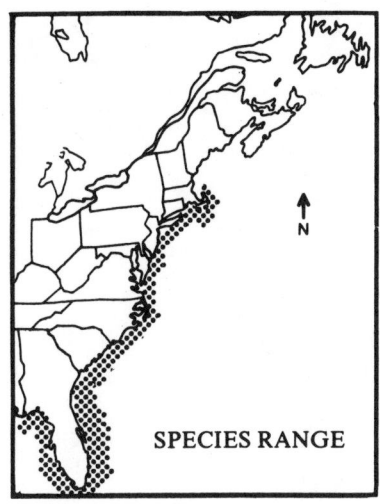

LITTLE TUNA
Euthynnus alletteratus

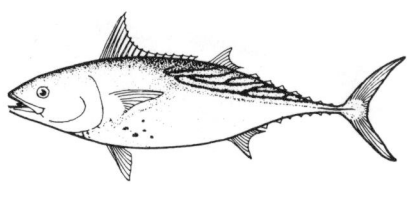

LITTLE TUNA, *Euthynnus alletteratus*. False albacore, tuna, school tuna. Miscalled albacore. SIZE: To 26 lbs; avg. 11-15 lbs; over 20 lbs unusual. HABITS: Pelagic, schooling and migratory. These rapid swimmers usually occur in salt water but at times in brackish water. They travel in aggregations varying from three or four individuals to schools of many hundreds. SEASON: Late May or June—November; best fishing in September and October. FISHING METHODS: Most are caught by trolling and casting from boats in water warmer than 65°F. BAITS: Feathers, stripbait, feather-stripbait or skirt-stripbait combination, spoons, jigs and plugs.

NOTES / NOTES

DATE	LOCATION	BAIT	COMMENTS

SPANISH MACKEREL
Scomberomorus maculatus

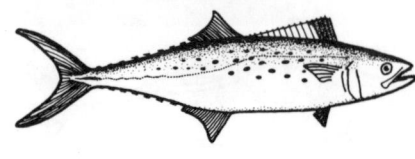

SPECIES RANGE

SPANISH MACKEREL, *Scomberomorus maculatus*. Mackerel. Distinguished from king mackerel by the scaleless pectoral fins and the lateral line sloping downward gradually under the 2nd dorsal fin. King mackerel have scaled pectoral fins and the lateral line dips downward abruptly under the 2nd dorsal fin. See cero mackerel. SIZE: To 12 lbs; avg. ½-1½ lbs; over 5 lbs unusual. HABITS: Pelagic and schooling. Occur throughout the water column to depths of 80 ft in water warmer than 67°F. Spanish mackerel will pursue bait fish through inlets into estuaries. SEASON: All year; best fishing October—April. FISHING METHODS: Casting, live lining, bottom fishing, jigging and chumming from shore; these methods plus trolling from boats. Most fish are caught within 2 miles of the beach and in or around inlets. Check state regulation on size limit. BAITS: Spoons, feathers, stripbait, weighted bucktails, plugs and jigs; also live shrimp or live fish and cut fish.

NOTES   NOTES

DATE	LOCATION	BAIT	COMMENTS

KING MACKEREL
Scomberomorus cavalla

SPECIES RANGE

KING MACKEREL, *Scomberomorus cavalla*. Kingfish, kings. Small ones are called snakes, large ones smokers. See Spanish mackerel and cero mackerel. SIZE: Largest recorded 103 lbs; tackle record 78¾ lbs; avg. 6-12 lbs; over 50 lbs unusual. HABITS: Pelagic and schooling. King mackerel occur over any type of bottom in salt water warmer than 67°F. Often congregate over wrecks, high relief rock or coral bottom and around buoys. Although some occasionally venture close enough to shore to be caught from ocean piers, most occur offshore of the 50 ft bottom contour. SEASON: All year; best fishing mid—October—April. FISHING METHODS: Live lining, casting, jigging, chumming and kite fishing from shore; these methods plus trolling from boats. Check state regulation on size limit. BAITS: Spoons, feathers, stripbait, feather-stripbait or skirt-stripbait combination, weighted bucktails, jigs and plugs; also shrimp, whole rigged mullet or ballyhoo, and live fish.

NOTES   NOTES

DATE	LOCATION	BAIT	COMMENTS

SKIPJACK TUNA
Katsuwonus pelamis

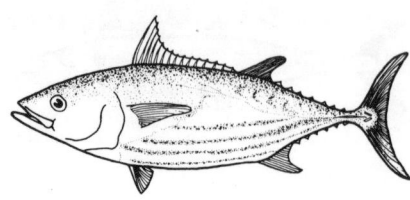

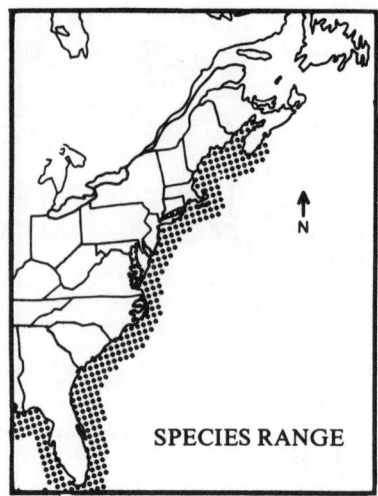

SPECIES RANGE

SKIPJACK TUNA, *Katsuwonus pelamis*. Oceanic bonito, arctic bonito, watermelon tuna. SIZE: To 45 lbs; tackle record 39 lbs 15 oz; avg. 3-5 lbs; over 15 lbs unusual. HABITS: Pelagic, schooling and migratory. These rapid swimmers usually occur near the surface in continental-shelf and oceanic water warmer than 63°F, but offshore of the 90 ft bottom contour. SEASON: All year; best fishing December—May. FISHING METHODS: Most are caught offshore by trolling near the surface in water of 68°-74°F. Also caught by casting from boats. BAITS: Feathers, stripbait, feather-stripbait or skirt-stripbait combination, spoons, jigs and plugs.

NOTES / NOTES

DATE	LOCATION	BAIT	COMMENTS

SCUP

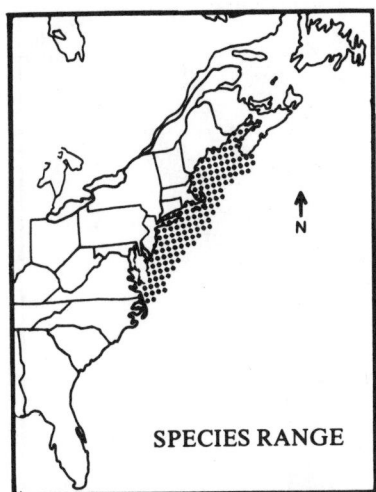

SPECIES RANGE

Stenotomus chrysops

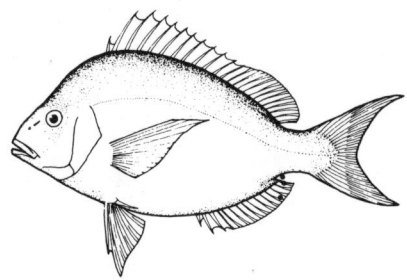

SCUP, *Stenotomus chrysops*. Porgy, Nelly Hunt, fair maid. SIZE: Largest recorded 5 lbs; avg. ¼ — ⅓ lb; over ¾ lb unusual. HABITS: Migratory and gregarious. Occur on sand, gravel or rock bottom and around shellfish beds, pilings or wrecks in the lower part of the Bay. Usually near bottom during daylight but move towards mid-depths at night. SEASON: May—October. Scup are never abundant and taken incidentally with other bottom fishes. FISHING METHODS: Bottom fishing, live lining and chumming from anchored or drifting boats. Some taken while bottom fishing from shore. BAITS: Clams, mussels, shrimp, worms, squid, cut fish, silversides and killifish.

NOTES   NOTES

DATE	LOCATION	BAIT	COMMENTS

SHEEPSHEAD
Archosargus probatocephalus

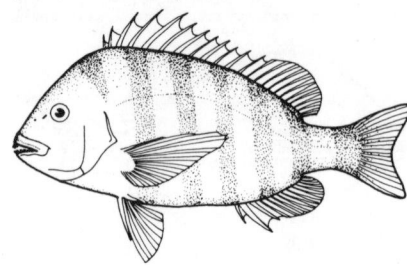

SPECIES RANGE

SHEEPSHEAD, *Archosargus probatocephalus*. Sheephead. SIZE: To 30 lbs; avg. 3-6 lbs; over 15 lbs unusual. HABITS: Aggregate in salt and brackish water on sand, shell, gravel or rock bottom and around jetties, breakwaters, rock piles and wrecks. SEASON: Late May—October. Owing to their small numbers and the skill required to hook them, sheepshead are taken only occasionally. FISHING METHODS: Most are caught by bottom fishing and chumming from boats or shore; some by jigging from boats. BAITS: Crabs, clams, mussels, shrimp and sand bugs; also small jigs and weighted bucktails.

NOTES

DATE	LOCATION	BAIT	COMMENTS

REDFISH

Sebastes marinus

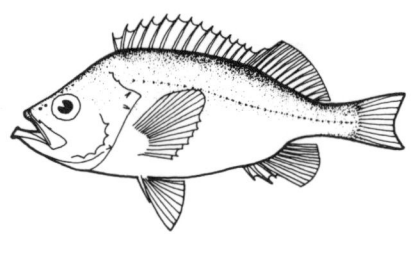

REDFISH, *Sebastes marinus*. Ocean perch, rosefish. SIZE: Largest recorded 19 lbs; avg. 1/3-1 lb; over 4 lbs unusual. HABITS: Gregarious. Occur in water of 32° to 60°F from the tide-line inshore to depth of at least 2,000 ft. During daylight they are found on rocky or other hard bottom and mud but rarely sand; at night they move towards mid-depths. SEASON: Can be taken all year in depths over 300 ft. East of Penobscot Bay taken in shallow water spring and fall and in deep water during the summer. South and west of Penobscot Bay taken in shallow water during the winter and in deep water the rest of the year. FISHING METHODS: Bottom fishing, live lining and jigging from boats. Taken from shore by these same methods around Eastport, Maine. BAITS: Shrimp, clams, mussels, worms, cut fish and small jigs.

NOTES   NOTES

DATE	LOCATION	BAIT	COMMENTS

ATLANTIC SALMON
Salmo salar

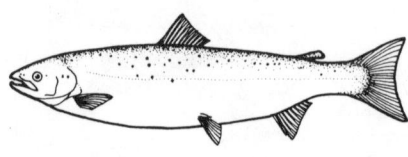

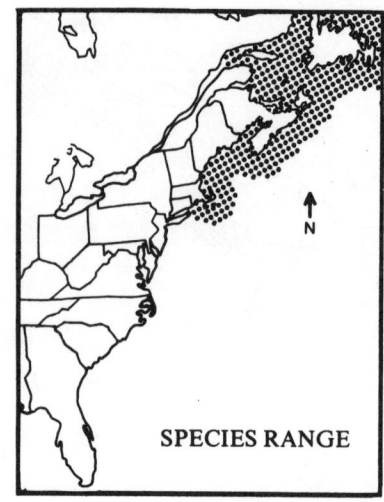

SPECIES RANGE

ATLANTIC SALMON, *Salmo salar*. Salmon, Atlantic sea-run salmon, Atlantics. Fish during various growth stages prior to first spawning are called smolt, grilse and salmon. Fish after spawning called kelts, slinks or black salmon. SIZE: Largest recorded in the western North Atlantic 60 lbs; avg. 8-12 lbs; over 20 lbs unusual. HABITS: Pelagic, schooling, anadromous. Salmon spend most of their lives in the ocean within 300 ft of the surface but migrate to fresh water to spawn. Unlike Pacific salmon which die after spawning once, Atlantic salmon return to the sea and may spawn as many as 4 times. During the spawning runs they feed very little, if at all, but will strike artificial flies. SEASON: Runs vary from year to year and stream to stream. Early runs occur from mid May—late June and late runs from mid July—mid September. Check state regulations on tackle, catch limits and season. FISHING METHODS: Anglers cast from shore or boats for salmon mostly in tidal waters of rivers and river mouths during the spawning migration. BAITS: Dry, wet and streamer flies.

NOTES   NOTES

DATE	LOCATION	BAIT	COMMENTS

SPINY DOGFISH
Squalus acanthias

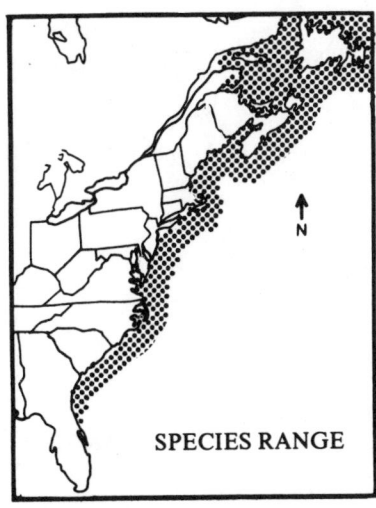

SPECIES RANGE

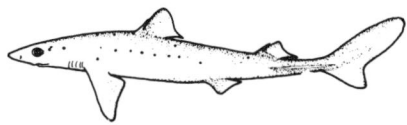

SPINY DOGFISH, *Squalus acanthias*. Dogfish, horndog, dog. SIZE: Largest recorded 20 lbs; avg. 4-7 lbs; over 15 lbs unusual. HABITS: Migratory and gregarious. Occur from the surface to depth of 800 ft or more in water of 39° to 62°F. However, usually on or near bottom of any type. Aggregations may be compact or scattered but are usually made up of similar size fish. These sharks are always moving and may erratically appear and disappear from an area. SEASON: Date of arrival varies from year to year ranging from April off southern Cape Cod to July at Eastport, Maine, but usually throughout the Gulf of Maine by late June. They depart in September or October. Most are caught by anglers in depths of 10 to 300 ft. FISHING METHODS: Bottom fishing, live lining, chumming and jigging from shore and boats. BAITS: Any natural bait; some taken on jigs.

NOTES

DATE	LOCATION	BAIT	COMMENTS

SMOOTH DOGFISH
Mustelus canis

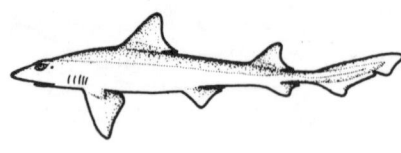

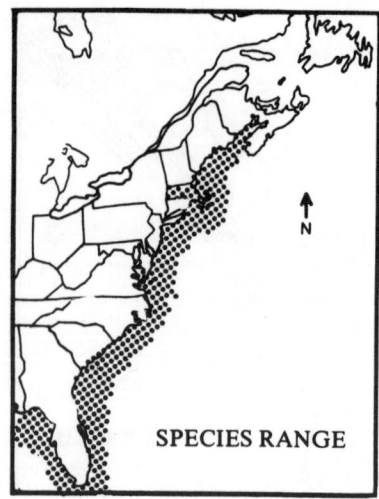

SPECIES RANGE

SMOOTH DOGFISH, *Mustelus canis*. Shark, dogfish, gray dog, smooth dog, miscalled sand shark. Distinguished from other sharks by the two spineless triangular dorsal fins of nearly the same size; rounded flat snout; 5th gill opening behind origin of pectoral fin and small, flat teeth. SIZE: To 20 lbs; avg. 1-4 lbs; over 10 lbs unusual. HABITS: Migratory. Occur from the tideline to depths of 600 ft or more in water of 43° to 72°F. Often found on or a few feet above any type of bottom along the open ocean shore or in estuaries; occasionally in fresh water. More active during night than day. SEASON: Early or mid May—early December. Most abundant during June in depths less than 60 ft. FISHING METHODS: Bottom fishing from shore or boats. BAITS: Squid, crabs, worms and cut fish.

NOTES

DATE	LOCATION	BAIT	COMMENTS

SAND SHARK
Carcharias taurus

SPECIES RANGE

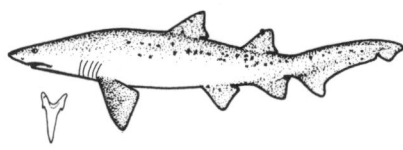

SAND SHARK, *Carcharias taurus*. Shark, ground shark. Distinguished from other sharks by the triangular dorsal fins of equal size, pointed snout, 5th gill opening in front of origin of pectoral fin and sharply pointed teeth. SIZE: To 400 lbs; avg. 15-40 lbs; over 275 lbs unusual. HABITS: Migratory. A sluggish shark occuring mostly on or a few feet above the bottom; many venture to the tide-line and some enter river mouths. More active during night than day. SEASON: Late May—November; best fishing late June—early October. Most taken in depths less than 30 ft. FISHING METHODS: Bottom fishing, live lining and chumming from shore or boats. A few caught while casting from shore at night. BAITS: Squid, crabs, clams, worms and any cut fish.

NOTES

DATE	LOCATION	BAIT	COMMENTS

BLUE SHARK
Prionace glauca

SPECIES RANGE

BLUE SHARK, *Prionace glauca*. Shark. Distinguished from other sharks by the long pointed snout, the long sickle-shaped pectoral fin and the 1st dorsal fin originating well behind the pectoral fin. SIZE: To 500 lbs; tackle record 410 lbs; avg. 125-225 lbs; over 300 lbs unusual. HABITS: Migratory. A pelagic shark ranging far out at sea, although they occasionally venture close inshore. Frequently seen at the surface swimming lazily or basking in the sun. SEASON: Early June—mid December; best fishing September—October. Most taken from the upper 60 ft in depths of 120-200 ft. FISHING METHODS: Trolling and chumming from boats. BAITS: Whole or cut fish. Occasionally taken on artificial lures.

NOTES   NOTES

DATE	LOCATION	BAIT	COMMENTS

SANDBAR SHARK
Carcharhinus milberti

SANDBAR SHARK, *Carcharhinus milberti*. Shark, brown shark, ground shark. Distinguished from other sharks by the large first dorsal fin (vertical height exceeds 10% of total body length) originating over the middle of equally large pectoral fin, and by a distinct ridge along the back between the dorsal fins. SIZE: To 230 lbs; small ones avg. 30-50 lbs, large ones 120-160 lbs; over 200 lbs unusual. HABITS: Migratory. A bottom dweller common both inshore and offshore but usually seen at the surface only when crossing a shoal area or when chummed to the surface. Adult females enter bays in early summer to give birth to their young. Large males remain offshore and are seldom seen at this time. A newborn sandbar shark is about 2 ft long and weighs 2½ lbs. SEASON: June—October; best fishing August—September. FISHING METHODS: Most adult sharks are caught in depths from 60 to 150 ft by bottom fishing or chumming; young sharks in bays by bottom fishing. BAITS: Cut or whole fish, clams, crabs, eels and squid.

NOTES

DATE	LOCATION	BAIT	COMMENTS

AMERICAN SMELT
Osmerus mordax

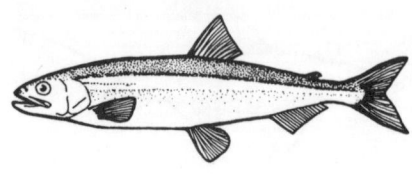
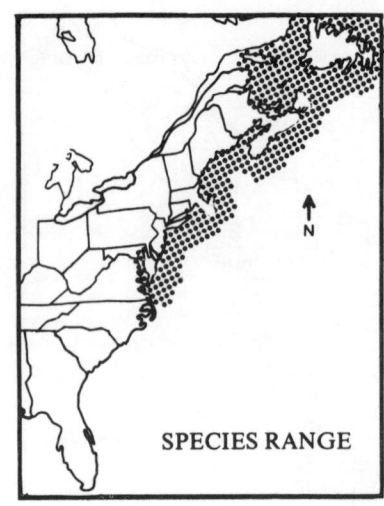

SPECIES RANGE

AMERICAN SMELT, *Osmerus mordax*. Smelt. SIZE: To 13 oz, avg. 1-4 oz, over 10 oz unusual. HABITS: Pelagic, schooling, anadromous. Feeding ceases during the spawning run in late winter and early spring. Inshore fish that spends nearly all of its life in or near the estuary of its natal stream or river. Spawning occurs in fresh or slightly brackish water streams usually a short distance above tidewater; sometimes in tidewater if obstructions bar upstream movement. Occur from the surface to 30 ft. SEASON: Taken all year, best fishing March—April and October—December. FISHING METHODS: Taken with hand dip-nets from shore throughout the spawning run; while live lining or jigging from shore or boats the rest of the year. Check state and local laws governing seasons and net fishing in your area. BAITS: Worms, shrimp, clams, silversides and killifish also small spoons, spinners and wet or streamer flies.

NOTES   NOTES

DATE	LOCATION	BAIT	COMMENTS

ATLANTIC WOLFFISH
Anarhichas lupus

SPECIES RANGE

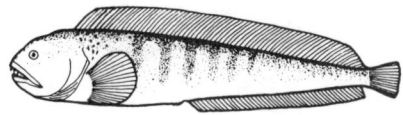

ATLANTIC WOLFFISH, *Anarhichas lupus*. Catfish, sea catfish, ocean catfish, wolffish. SIZE: Largest recorded 40 lbs; average 7-13 lbs; over 25 lbs unusual. HABITS: Solitary and sedentary. Occur in water of 31° to 52°F. Wolffish favor a high relief bottom such as rock outcrops or large stones with intervening mud and sand. Occur from a few feet below the tideline inshore to over 500 ft offshore. SEASON: Can be taken throughout the year in depths over 180 ft and during summer in shallower water. FISHING METHODS: Bottom fishing and jigging from anchored or slow-drifting boats. BAITS: Clams, whelks, crabs, cut fish and diamond jigs.

NOTES

DATE	LOCATION	BAIT	COMMENTS

CUNNER

Tautogolabrus adspersus

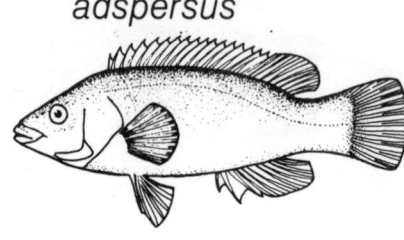

SPECIES RANGE

CUNNER, *Tautogolabrus adspersus*. Choggie, bait stealer. Distinguished from tautog by a pointed snout and a scaled gill cover. Tautog have a blunt snout and a scaleless gill cover. SIZE: To 3½ lbs; avg. ¼-½ lb; over 1½ lbs unusual. HABITS: Gregarious, year-round resident. Occur on rocky or other hard bottom and around shellfish beds from the tide-line to 350 ft, rarely to 400 ft. At times on soft bottom. Cunner frequent wrecks, jetties, breakwaters, pilings and wharves. Feed during daylight. SEASON: Taken all year in depths over 120 ft; April—November in shallower water. Best fishing June—October in depths from 5 to 60 ft. FISHING METHODS: Live lining or bottom fishing from shore or boats. BAITS: Clams, worms, mussels, shrimp and cut fish; also small spoons, spinners and weighted bucktails.

NOTES

DATE	LOCATION	BAIT	COMMENTS

SPECIES RANGE

TAUTOG

Tautoga onitis

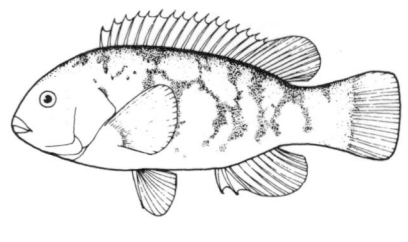

TAUTOG, *Tautoga onitis*. Blackfish, tog, Molly George, chub. SIZE: To 22½ lbs; tackle record 21½ lbs; avg. 1-4 lbs; over 13 lbs unusual. HABITS: These gregarious year-round residents live in salt water but occasionally enter brackish water. Occur on rock, gravel, shell or sand bottom and around wrecks, jetties, breakwaters, stone piles, bridge abutments or pilings. Active from the tide-line to depths of at least 120 ft, especially in water of 46° — 65°F; inactive when the water temperature is less than 46°F. SEASON: All year; best fishing in October and November. FISHING METHODS: Bottom fishing from shore or anchored boats. Most abundant fish in catches made by underwater spear fishermen. BAITS: Clams, worms, mussels, shrimp, crabs and sand bugs.

NOTES   NOTES

DATE	LOCATION	BAIT	COMMENTS

NORTHERN PUFFER
Sphaeroides maculatus

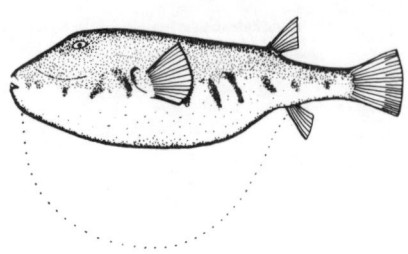
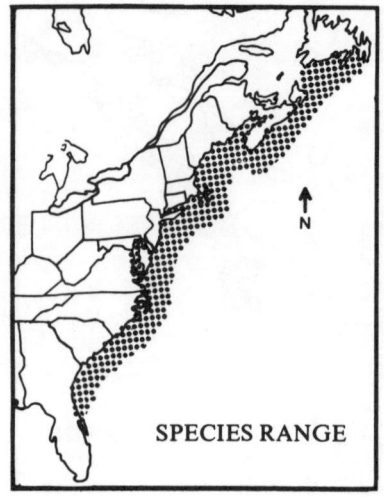

SPECIES RANGE

NORTHERN PUFFER, *Sphaeroides maculatus*. Blow toad, swell toad, blowfish, swellfish. SIZE: To 2½ lbs; avg. ⅓ — ⅔ lb; over 1½ lbs unusual HABITS: Aggregate on or a few feet above mud, sand, shell or gravel bottom in salt or brackish water. Abundance fluctuates yearly. Puffers have the ability to inflate themselves with water or air as a self-defense mechanism. SEASON: April or May—October or early November; best fishing late April—early June. FISHING METHODS: Bottom fishing from anchored or drifting boats and shore. BAITS: Worms, clams, mussels, shrimp, squid, small crabs, silversides, killifish and cut fish.

NOTES

DATE	LOCATION	BAIT	COMMENTS

SWORDFISH

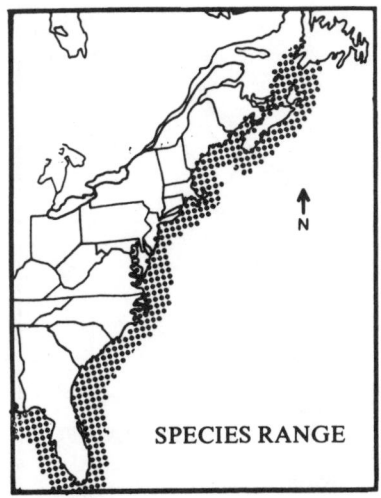

Xiphias gladius

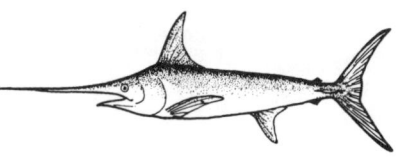

SWORDFISH, *Xiphias gladius*. Broadbill, broadbill swordfish. SIZE: Largest recorded in the Atlantic Ocean 1,100 lbs; largest taken on tackle in Western North Atlantic 602 lbs; (World tackle record 1,182 lbs caught in Pacific Ocean off Chile); average 200-300 lbs; over 450 lbs unusual. HABITS: Pelagic and migratory. Occur in oceanic and continental-shelf water from the surface to depths of 2,100 ft or more. SEASON: Taken mid June—September; best fishing July—August. Most now caught 20 to 50 miles offshore when the surface temperature of the water is warmer than 58° to 60°F. In the past swordfish were common a few miles from the coast. FISHING METHODS: Boat anglers usually sight fish at the surface before presenting the bait; some fish taken while blind trolling or chumming. BAITS: Whole squid, mackerel, eel, silver hake and mullet.

NOTES

DATE	LOCATION	BAIT	COMMENTS

COBIA

Rachycentron canadum

SPECIES RANGE

COBIA, *Rachycentron canadum*. Crab-eater, sergeant fish, ling. Sometimes miscalled bonito or black bonito. SIZE: To 120 lbs; tackle record 102 lbs; avg. 20-30 lbs; over 75 lbs unusual. HABITS: Migratory. Cobia, occuring both inshore and offshore, are usually solitary or in small groups and often found around buoys, wrecks, debris, rock piles and pilings. Sometimes they are associated with either fish schools, sea turtles or large rays. SEASON: May—mid October; best fishing late June—August. FISHING METHODS: Bottom fishing, live lining, casting, chumming or trolling from boats. BAITS: Whole eel, spot and shedder crab or cut fish; also spoons, plugs and large weighted bucktails.

NOTES   NOTES

DATE	LOCATION	BAIT	COMMENTS

DOLPHIN

SPECIES RANGE

Coryphaena hippurus

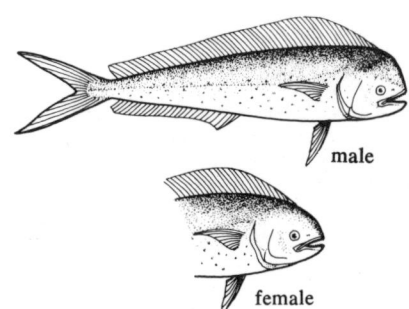

male

female

DOLPHIN, *Coryphaena hippurus*. Small ones called school dolphin; large males called bulls. SIZE: To 85 lbs; tackle record 85 lbs; avg. 3-7 lbs; over 45 lbs unusual. HABITS: Pelagic, schooling and migratory. These rapid swimmers occur near the surface in water warmer than 70°F. Although dolphin occasionally venture close enough to shore to be caught from ocean piers, they usually occur offshore of the 60 ft bottom contour. They often gather under floating debris and seaweed and around buoys. SEASON: Most are caught from March—November, but some all year within the Gulf Stream. Best fishing is in July and August. FISHING METHODS: Trolling or casting from boats. Most are caught 8 or more miles offshore. BAITS: Feathers, spoons, jigs, plugs, weighted bucktails, stripbait, feather-stripbait or skirt-stripbait combination, and whole rigged mullet, ballyhoo, squid or mackerel.

NOTES   NOTES

DATE	LOCATION	BAIT	COMMENTS

ATLANTIC SPADEFISH
Chaetodipterus faber

SPECIES RANGE

ATLANTIC SPADEFISH, *Chaetodipterus faber*. Spadefish, angelfish. SIZE: To 16 lbs; avg. ⅓-1 lb; over 5 lbs unusual. HABITS: Aggregate in salt water on sand, shell, coral or rock bottom and around buoys, wrecks, rock piles, bridge abutments, pilings, jetties and breakwaters. They usually occur inshore of the 90 ft bottom contour. SEASON: All year. FISHING METHODS: Bottom fishing from boats or shore. BAITS: Clams, worms, shrimp, crabs and cut fish.

NOTES — NOTES

DATE	LOCATION	BAIT	COMMENTS

GREAT BARRACUDA
Sphyraena barracuda

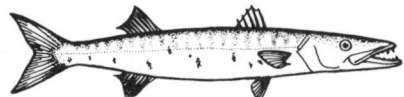

GREAT BARRACUDA, *Sphyraena barracuda*. Barracuda, cuda. SIZE: Largest recorded 106 lbs; tackle record 83 lbs; avg. 7-13 lbs; over 40 lbs unusual. HABITS: Pelagic and migratory. Occur both offshore and inshore over any type of bottom. Barracuda often concentrate around wrecks or rock and coral bottom with high relief. SEASON: All year; best fishing May—September or early October. Most are caught near the surface in water from near shore to about 100 ft deep and temperatures warmer than 70°F. FISHING METHODS: Live lining, chumming, and casting from shore; these methods plus trolling from boats. Usually taken incidentally while fishing for other species. BAITS: Stripbait and cut fish or live shrimp, pinfish, ballyhoo, mullet and snapper; also spoons, plugs, jigs and weighted bucktails.

NOTES

DATE	LOCATION	BAIT	COMMENTS

BONEFISH

Albula vulpes

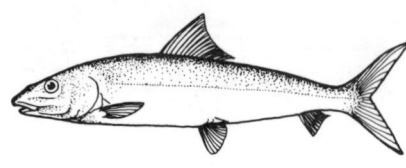

SPECIES RANGE

BONEFISH, *Albula vulpes*. Silver ghost, phantom. SIZE: To over 20 lbs; tackle record 19 lbs; avg. 4-6 lbs; over 12 lbs unusual. HABITS: These inshore fish occur singly, in groups or in schools from the tide-line to depths of 40 ft. They often feed by rooting in the bottom of sand and grass flats; this feeding action is called "tailing" or "mudding." SEASON: All year; best fishing is during June. FISHING METHODS: Chumming, live lining and casting from boats or while wading in shallow water. Most bonefish are caught in depths of ½-10 feet. BAITS: Shrimp, crabs, clams, conch, sand bugs and squid; also weighted bucktails, feathers, plugs and streamer flies.

NOTES

DATE	LOCATION	BAIT	COMMENTS

SEA CATFISH
Galeichthys felis

SPECIES RANGE

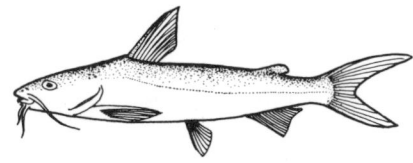

SEA CATFISH, *Galeichthys felis.* Sea cat, catfish. SIZE: To 3 lbs; avg. ⅓— ⅔ lb; over 1½ lbs unusual. HABITS: These shallow water shore fish aggregate on any type of bottom. Although small ones occur in both salt and brackish water, large ones are almost always in salt water. More active during night than day. SEASON: All year; best fishing April—November. FISHING METHODS: Bottom fishing from shore or boats. Most are caught incidentally while fishing for other species. BAITS: Shrimp, crabs, cut fish and squid.

NOTES

DATE	LOCATION	BAIT	COMMENTS

GAFFTOPSAIL CATFISH
Bagre marinus

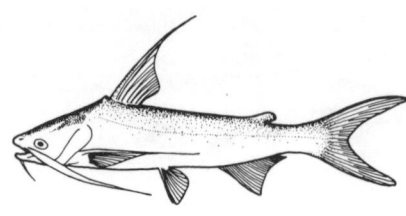

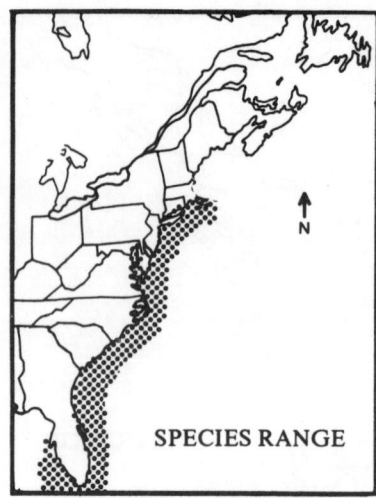

SPECIES RANGE

GAFFTOPSAIL CATFISH, *Bagre marinus.* Sail cat, top cat, catfish. SIZE: To 6 lbs; avg. ¾—1½ lbs; over 3 lbs unusual. HABITS: These inshore fish occur on any type of bottom in salt and brackish water, some in nearly fresh water. Although primarily bottom feeders, they sometimes pursue prey to the surface. Unlike sea catfish, gafftopsail catfish strike artificial lures. More active during night than day. SEASON: All year; best fishing April—November. FISHING METHODS: Bottom fishing or casting from shore or boats. BAITS: Shrimp, crabs, cut fish and squid; also weighted bucktails, plugs and streamer flies.

NOTES   NOTES

DATE	LOCATION	BAIT	COMMENTS

WHITE GRUNT
Haemulon plumieri

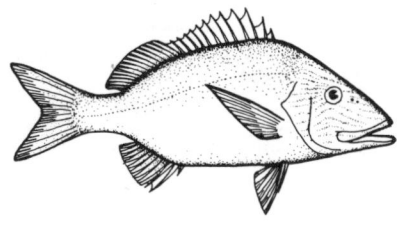

WHITE GRUNT, *Haemulon plumieri*. Grunt, common grunt. Miscalled scup. Distinguished from pigfish by its large mouth having an orange-red lining, and by its body scales larger above the lateral line than those below it. In contrast, pigfish have a small mouth with no bright color inside, and its body scales above the lateral line are about the same size as those below. SIZE: To 4 lbs; avg. ⅓–⅔ lb; over 2 lbs unusual. HABITS: Occur in salt and brackish water on mud, sand, rock or coral bottom and around wrecks, piers, jetties or bridge abutments. Although common in estuaries, inlets and along ocean beaches, they occur offshore in depths of 100 ft or more. They usually feed within a few feet of the bottom. SEASON: All year; best fishing is during July and August. FISHING METHODS: Bottom fishing and jigging from shore or boats. BAITS: Shrimp, crabs, worms, clams and cut fish; also small weighted bucktails and jigs.

NOTES   NOTES

DATE	LOCATION	BAIT	COMMENTS

PIGFISH

Orthopristis chrysoptera

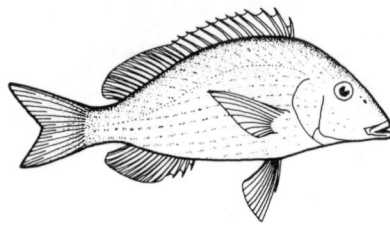

SPECIES RANGE

PIGFISH, *Orthopristis chrysoptera*. Grunt. Often miscalled hogfish and sailors choice. See white grunt. SIZE: To 2 lbs; avg. ¼-½ lb; over 1½ lbs unusual. HABITS: Occur in salt and brackish water on sand or mud bottom and around wrecks, piers, jetties or bridge abutments. Although common in estuaries, inlets and along ocean beaches, they also occur offshore to depths of 100 ft or more. Pigfish usually feed within a few feet of the bottom. SEASON: All year; best fishing April—September. FISHING METHODS: Bottom fishing and jigging from shore or boats. Although pigfish are plentiful, they are not highly sought. Most are caught incidentally with other bottom fishes. BAITS: Shrimp, crabs, squid, worms, clams, mussels and cut fish; also small weighted bucktails and jigs. Pigfish are often used as live or cut bait for other species.

NOTES NOTES

DATE	LOCATION	BAIT	COMMENTS

GREAT AMBERJACK
Seriola dumerili

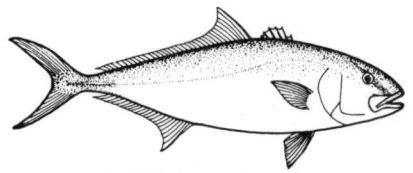

GREAT AMBERJACK, *Seriola dumerili*. Amberjack. SIZE: To over 180 lbs; tackle record 149 lbs; avg. 15-25 lbs; over 100 lbs unusual. HABITS: These fast swimmers occur in schools in oceanic and continental-shelf water from the surface to depths of at least 1,000 ft. Although great amberjack may occur anywhere in the water column, they often concentrate over high relief rock or coral bottom and around wrecks or buoys. SEASON: Most are caught from March—November; best fishing in July and August. FISHING METHODS: Trolling, bottom fishing, jigging, chumming and live lining from boats. Anglers catch many large amberjack while fishing for snappers and groupers in depths of 90-300 ft. BAITS: Live and dead fish; also stripbait, plugs, spoons, feathers and jigs.

NOTES   NOTES

DATE	LOCATION	BAIT	COMMENTS

CREVALLE JACK
Caranx hippos

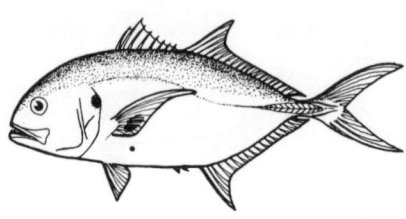

SPECIES RANGE

CREVALLE JACK, *Caranx hippos*. Jack, jack crevalle. **SIZE:** To over 70 lbs; avg. 1-3 lbs inshore, 7-12 lbs offshore; over 25 lbs unusual. **HABITS:** Pelagic and schooling. These rapid swimmers occur in salt and brackish water; sometimes in coastal rivers to nearly fresh water. Occur over any type of bottom, but congregate over wrecks and high relief rock or coral bottom. Small fish are common in shallow estuaries; as they grow larger, they tend to move offshore into deeper water. **SEASON:** All year; best fishing mid March—November. **FISHING METHODS:** Casting, jigging, live lining, chumming and bottom fishing from shore; these methods plus trolling from boats. **BAITS:** Feathers, spoons, plugs, jigs, weighted bucktails and bucktail flies; also live or cut fish and shrimp.

NOTES   NOTES

DATE	LOCATION	BAIT	COMMENTS

POMPANO

Trachinotus carolinus

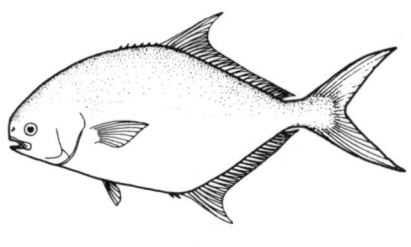

POMPANO, *Trachinotus carolinus*. This fish is more commonly referred to as the pompano than any of its other Atlantic coast relatives. See permit and palometa. SIZE: To 8 lbs; avg. 1-2 lbs; over 5 lbs unusual. HABITS: These schooling fish are caught along ocean beaches, in estuaries and in inlets. Adults leave shallow water seasonally to spawn offshore, some as far as 60 miles from land. Pompano feed on or a few feet off sand and mud bottom in water warmer than 65°F. Many die when trapped in water colder than 60°F. SEASON: All year; best fishing November—May. FISHING METHODS: Bottom fishing, casting, live lining, chumming and jigging from shore; these methods plus trolling from boats. Check state regulation on size limit. BAITS: Shrimp, sand bugs, cut fish and clams; also small weighted bucktails, jigs and feathers.

NOTES   NOTES

DATE	LOCATION	BAIT	COMMENTS

Glossary

ANADROMOUS. Spoken of fish which spend most of their lives in salt or brackish water but ascend rivers to spawn in slightly brackish or fresh water.

BERTH. A place at a dock or wharf where a boat is tied.

BOBBING. A method of fishing for eels. A number of earthworms are threaded on cotton twine and then made into a ball. The ball is usually attached to a short length of line on the end of a cane pole. When an eel takes this bait it tangles its teeth on the twine and is caught.

BOTTOM CONTOUR. An imaginary line on the floor of a body of water connecting points of equal depth.

BOTTOM FISHING. Placing a bait on or near the bottom so as to catch fish. The bait, usually weighted with a sinker, may be cast and allowed to sink or it may be lowered vertically into the water. Sometimes the bait is buoyed by a float so that it remains suspended just off the bottom. The bait is left in place until a fish bites or until the angler slowly retrieves it.

BRACKISH WATER. Applied in this book to water having from 0.2 to 17 parts per thousand, by weight, of dissolved salts.

BREACHWAY. A term used in Rhode Island for an inlet.

BROKEN BOTTOM. A rough, stony or rocky area of the sea floor.

BUOY. A float moored to the bottom to mark a channel or to warn of an obstruction or other danger. Special-purpose buoys are often used to mark the location of artificial fishing reefs.

CASTING. Throwing forth a bait. The bait, either a natural one or artificial lure made to imitate a natural one, is attached to one end of a line, the other end is attached to the angler's reel. When the bait or lure strikes the water, the angler can rapidly retrieve it, let it drift with the current, or let it sink to the bottom. *See* Squidding, Live Lining and Bottom Fishing.

CATADROMOUS. Spoken of fish which spend most of their lives in fresh or brackish water but spawn in salt water.

CHARTER BOAT. A fishing boat with crew hired for the exclusive use of one to six anglers. With the advice of the captain, the anglers determine what type of fishing they will do. Charter boats range in size from a small outboard with guide ($20 or more per day) to a twin-engine, ocean-going vessel in excess of 50 feet with a captain and two mates ($150 or more per day). Tackle and bait are usually furnished with the boat. *See* Party Boats.

CHUMMING. Attracting fish to an area with fish or shellfish, either ground, chopped, or whole, or sometimes with scrap meat and dried blood. Once fish are in the area, hooks baited with cut and whole fish or artificial lures are used to catch them. *See* Live Lining and Bottom Fishing. Oily fish such as menhaden, herring, shad and mackerel are usually used for chum. Chumming for bottom fish is done by lowering a porous container filled with chum. This may be a punctured can of pet food, a wire basket or pot (chum pot), or a cloth bag (chum bag).

COASTAL. Spoken of marine fishes which spend most of their lives within a few miles of shore.

CONTINENTAL SHELF. A submarine plain extending out from shore to a depth of about 600 feet, beyond which the ocean bottom begins a relatively steep descent to the deep ocean floor.

CUT. A term used in southern Florida for an inlet.

DIAMOND JIG. An elongated, narrow, diamond-shaped jig. Weights usually range from ½ ounce to 2½ pounds.

DIP NET. Also called hand dip net. A conical, small-mesh net attached to a rigid frame on a long handle. It is used to catch fish or crabs. Along the southeast coast the term dip net usually applies to a rectangular, small-mesh net supported by a metal frame and attached to a rope or pole. Here it is used to catch baitfish and shrimp.

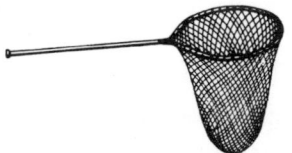 

DRY FLY. An artificial fly designed to float on the water. *See* Fly.

ESTUARY. A partially enclosed body of water having a free connection with the open ocean, within which salt and fresh water mix.

FEATHER. Also called a trolling feather. An artificial bait or lure made to simulate a baitfish and used for trolling. The feather is made of a round or bullet-shaped metal head to which is attached a feather, hair, nylon or other synthetic material body.

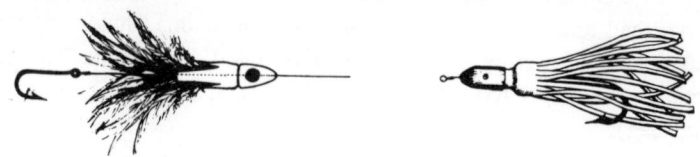

FIRE LIGHTING. Also called night lighting, gigging and floundering. Locating or attracting fish in shallow water at night with lights either held above or below the surface. Once a fish is located, it is usually speared.

FLAT. A low-relief plane at the border between a body of water and land. The flat is alternately exposed and submerged, according to the tide. It is designated according to its surface characteristics, as mud flat, sand flat, grass flat, etc.

FLATLINE. A trolling line fished directly astern of a boat.

FLOAT-RIG. Also called popping-jig in southern Florida. A floating plug to which is attached a hook baited with a live fish or shrimp. The plug splashes and makes a popping noise as the rig is drawn through the water, and this disturbance attracts fish to the bait. Float-rigs are often used to catch spotted sea trout.

FLOUNDERING. Fire lighting specifically for flatfishes. *See* Fire Lighting.

FLY. A lightweight artificial bait or lure made to simulate a live insect or other small natural bait. The fly consists of a hook dressed with feathers, hair, yarn and tinsel and tied with thread. *See* Dry Fly, Wet Fly and Streamer Fly.

FRESH WATER. Applied in this book to water having less than 0.2 parts per thousand, by weight, of dissolved salts.

GIGGING. Fishing with a spear, especially while fire lighting.

GULF STREAM. Also called the Stream. A general term used to describe the narrow, relatively fast-flowing ocean current along the Atlantic coast of North America. Properly called the Gulf Stream System, it is made up principally of the Florida Current and the Antilles Current. The name Gulf Stream is based on the misconception that the current's source is the Gulf of Mexico.

HEADLAND. A high point of land or rock projecting into the sea.

INLET. A narrow passage of water connecting the open sea with protected coastal and inland water. Along various sections of our coast, inlets are called breachways, cuts and passes.

INSHORE. Referring to the part of the sea adjacent to the shore. In this book it is bound by the 60-foot bottom contour.

INTRACOASTAL WATERWAY. Also called Inland Waterway or Waterway. A comparatively shallow passage extending continuously on the Atlantic Seaboard from Manasquan, New Jersey, to Key West, Florida. Sheltered from the open sea, it consists of a series of artificial channels connecting bays, sounds, lagoons and other protected waters. It is used primarily by small craft.

JIG. An artificial lure made to simulate a live bait. Although many variations exist, all jigs are made wholly or partly of metal, hence, are heavy for their size. In weight they range from less than 1 ounce to over 2 pounds.

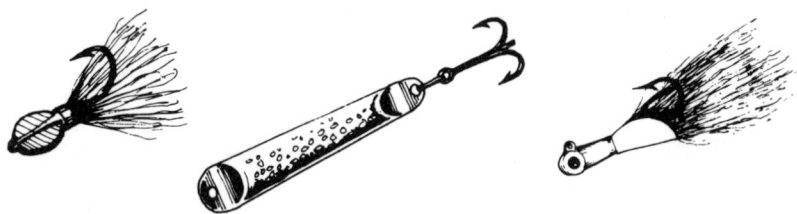

JIGGING. Manipulating an artificial lure to imitate a live bait and thus attract fish to the hook. The lure is lowered vertically or cast some distance away, allowed to sink to a desired depth, and then jerked quickly upward a short distance. Immediately after this upward jerk the lure is allowed to sink back. This jerking or jigging procedure is repeated again and again.

KEY. A low island or reef off the southern coast of Florida. This word is derived from the Spanish "cayo" meaning little island. In the West Indies, it is spelled Cay (pronounced ké or kā).

KITE FISHING. A method of fishing done by suspending a baitfish from a kite. When flown from a boat, the kite carries the bait well away from the boat's wake. Live fish are slowly trolled just under the surface. Dead fish may be fished this way, or skipped along the surface at a faster trolling speed. When flown from a beach, the kite carries the bait out a distance from shore. During periods of light breeze, helium-filled balloons are sometimes used in place of kites.

LIVE BAITING. Live lining with live bait.

LIVE BOTTOM. An area of the sea floor abounding in living attached organisms such as mussels, sponges, sea fans, live corals, sea weeds, etc.

LIVE LINING. Allowing a natural bait, either alive or dead, to drift in a current or be suspended by a float some distance above the bottom. As the bait drifts away from the angler, line must be played out from the unlocked spool or open bail of the reel. Live lining is often done while chumming. *See* Live Baiting.

MOORING. A float, usually a small buoy, anchored away from land to which a boat is tied.

MOP. An artificial bait or lure made to simulate a natural bait and trolled in the water. It consists of a small-linked brass chain 6 to 14 inches long with tufts of thread tied or glued into each link. Attached to the front of the chain is either a swivel or a weight, and to the rear end a hook. This lure is usually trolled.

NIGHT LIGHTING. *See* Fire Lighting.

OFFSHORE. Applied in this book to the part of the sea away from shore beyond about the 60 foot bottom contour.

OUTBOARD. A rowboat propelled by an outboard motor.

OUTRIGGERS. Movable rods or poles which project outward from each side of a boat and used during trolling to keep the baits spread apart.

PARTY BOAT. Also called head boat, open boat, ground-fishing boat, deep sea-fishing boat, drift-fishing boat, and packet or party packet. A fishing boat, usually carrying 10 to 60 anglers. Space is sold to the general public until either the boat is filled to capacity or the scheduled sailing time is reached. The captain usually determines the type of fishing and the areas to be fished. The fee ranges from $3 to $20, depending on duration of the trip or distance from port, and usually includes bait but not tackle. Trip lengths are usually eight hours for a full day, four hours for a half day. *See* Charter Boat.

PASS. A term used in the Florida Keys and along the coast of the Gulf of Mexico for an inlet. As used in the Florida Keys, it is the passageway from the sea to Florida Bay and ranges in width from a fraction of a mile to 7 miles.

PELAGIC. Spoken of fishes and other sea animals that are more or less independent of the bottom. They are characteristically active swimmers spending much of their time in mid-water or near the surface.

RELIEF. Used in this book to describe a sharp rise above or depression below the plane of the sea floor caused by an outcropping of rock or coral, submerged ridge, sunken ship, etc.

RIGGED BAIT. A natural bait consisting of all or part of a dead fish or squid which is tied, sewn or wired onto a hook and used for trolling.

 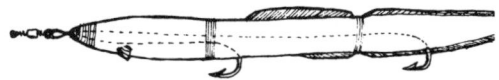

ROWBOAT. An open boat, usually 12 to 16 feet long, propelled by oars. The bottom may be flat, round, or V-shaped.

RUNABOUT. An open boat, usually 14 to 17 feet long, having a planing hull and powered by an outboard motor of 10 or more horsepower.

SALT WATER. Applied in this book to water having more than 17 parts per thousand, by weight, of dissolved salts. Average sea water for all oceans has about 35 parts per thousand of dissolved salts.

SCHOOL. A large number of fish, usually of the same kind and size, swimming and feeding together. The members are closely oriented to each other in such a way that the school behaves as a well integrated unit.

SHAD DART. A small jig, usually a weighted bucktail, weighing about ¼ ounce or less. Darts are used primarily to catch shad and similar fishes.

SKIFF. A boat, usually 18 to 26 feet long, propelled by an inboard or inboard-outboard motor.

SKIRT. An artificial bait or lure consisting of a brightly colored shredded plastic tube 4 to 8 inches long and fitted over a feather, stripbait, rigged bait or other trolling lure.

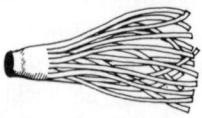

SPINNER. An artificial bait or lure composed of one or more spoon-like blades that spin on a shaft or swivel when drawn through the water. Presumably the glitter caused by the spinning blades' reflecting light simulates the metallic sheen of a baitfish; this acts together with vibrations emitted by the spinner in stimulating fish to bite.

SPOON. An artificial lure made to simulate a live bait. It usually consists of a thin, slightly curved piece of metal or combination of metal and plastic. When drawn through the water it has a wobbling and wiggling motion.

SQUIDDING. A term sometimes used to describe the casting into the surf of metal lures called squids.

STREAMER FLY. A wet fly, made on a long shank hook, designed to simulate a small baitfish. *See* Fly.

STRIPBAIT. A long narrow strip of skin and flesh cut from the sides or belly of a fish or squid in a shape simulating the outline of a whole fish. This strip is attached to a hook and used for trolling.

THERMOCLINE. A narrow zone in the water column where a sharp change in temperature occurs between relatively warm water above and cool water below.

TIDE-LINE. The water level at the shore, which changes with the tide.

TROLLING. Trailing a natural bait, artificial lure, or a combination of the two behind a moving boat. The bait can be made to skip along the water surface or troll at any depth below the surface to just above the bottom. A bait or lure trailed by an angler running along a fishing pier, bridge or breakwater is also trolling. Trolling speeds vary according to the fish species sought.

TUBE LURE. Also called surgical-tube lure, teaser, and Norwegian teaser. An artificial lure made to simulate a live bait. The lure consists of a hook covered by a piece of surgical or plastic tubing 3 to 12 inches long. Large tube lures are usually trolled; small ones are attached to a fishing line ahead of a diamond jig.

WATER COLUMN. Spoken of the water from surface to bottom about a given point.

WEIGHTED BUCKTAIL. A type of jig consisting of a lead or metal head cast on a single hook. The tail can be made of hair, nylon, feathers or other fibrous material.

WET FLY. An artificial fly designed to sink in the water. *See* Fly.

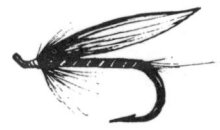

Index

Albacore, 55
Amberjack, 83
American shad, 49
American smelt, 68
Angelfish, 76
Arctic bonito, 58
Atlantic bonito, 54
Atlantic cod, 20
Atlantic croaker, 36
Atlantic halibut, 45
Atlantic mackerel, 51
Atlantic sailfish, 42
Atlantic salmon, 62
Atlantic spadefish, 76
Atlantic tomcod, 26
Atlantic wolffish, 69

Barracuda, 77
Bass, 8
Bay porgy, 59, 76
Big-eyed mackerel, 52
Billfish, 40
Blackback flounder, 43
Black bass, 10
Black bonito, 74
Black drum, 35
Blackfish, 10, 11, 71
Blackfin grouper, 17
Black grouper, 13, 14, 17
Black jewfish, 13
Black sea bass, 10
Blowfish, 72
Blow toad, 72
Bluefin tuna, 53
Bluefish, 19
Blue hake, 23
Blue marlin, 41
Blue perch, 70
Blue shark, 66
Bonefish 78,
Bonito, 51, 54, 74
Broadbill, 73
Broadbill swordfish, 73

Brown hake, 24
Brown shark, 67
Bulldrum, 34
Bullhead whiting, 30, 37, 39

Carolina whiting, 30, 37
Catfish, 69, 79, 80
Channel bass, 34
Chicken halibut, 45
Choggier, 70
Chub mackerel, 51, 52
Cobia, 74
Cod, 20
Codfish, 20
Common grunt, 81
Crab-eater, 74
Crevalle jack, 84
Croaker, 36
Cuda, 77
Cunner, 70
Cusk, 25

Dog, 63
Dogfish, 63, 64
Dolphin, 75
Drum, 29, 34, 35

Eel, freshwater, 28

False albacore, 55
Flounder, 43, 44, 46, 47, 48
Fluke, 46
Frostfish, 26

Gafftopsail catfish, 80
Gag grouper, 14, 17
Giant sea bass, 16
Giant tuna, 53
Gray dog, 64
Gray grouper, 14
Gray hake, 23
Gray mullet, 39
Gray sea trout, 29

Gray trout, 29
Great amberjack, 83
Great barracuda, 77
Ground shark, 65, 67
Grouper, 12, 13, 14, 15, 18
Grunt, 81, 82
Gulf kingfish, 39

Haddock, 22
Hake, 20, 23, 24
Halibut, 45
Harbor pollock, 21
Hardhead, 36, 52
Herring, 49
Hick, 50
Hickory shad, 50
Hogfish, 82
Horndog, 63

Jacks, 68, 83, 84
Jack crevalle, 84
Jewfish, 13, 16

Kingfish, 30, 37, 39
King mackerel, 57
King whiting, 30, 37, 39
Kitty Mitchell, 15

Lemon sole, 43
Ling 24, 74
Little tuna, 55

Mackerel, 51, 52
Marlin, 40
Mud hake, 24
Mullet, 30, 37, 39

Nassau grouper, 18
Northern fluke, 46
Northern kingfish, 30
Northern puffer, 72

Ocean catfish, 69
Oceanic bonito, 58
Ocean perch, 61

Pan trout, 29, 33
Perch, 9, 32, 70
Phantom, 78
Pigfish, 82
Pin, 59
Pollock, 20, 21
Pompano, 83, 85
Porgy, 59, 76
Puffer, 72
Puppy drum, 34

Red bass, 34
Red drum, 34
Redfish, 61
Red grouper, 12
Red hake, 24
Rock bass, 11
Rockfish, 61
Rock sea bass, 11
Rosefish, 61
Roundhead, 30, 37
Ruby red lips, 81

Sail cat, 80
Sailfish, 42
Sailors choice, 82
Salmon, 62
Sandbar shark, 67
Sand dab, 47
Sand flounder, 47
Sand perch, 32
Sand porgy, 59
Sand shark, 64, 65
Sand trout, 38
Scad, 83
School bass, 8, 34
School dolphin, 75
School tuna, 53
Scrod, 22

Scup, 59
Sea bass, 8, 10, 11, 34
Sea cat, 79
Sea catfish, 69, 79
Sea mackerel, 51
Sea mullet, 30, 37, 39
Sea perch, 9, 70
Sea pollock, 21
Sea porgy, 59
Sea-run salmon, 6
Sea trout, 29
Sergeant fish, 74
Shad, 49, 50
Shark, 63, 64, 65, 66, 67
Sheepshead, 60
Silver ghost, 78
Silver hake, 23, 27
Silver perch, 32
Silver sea trout, 29, 38
Silver trout, 38
Silver whiting, 39
Skipjack tuna, 58
Smelt, 68
Smooth dog, 64
Smooth dogfish, 64
Smooth flounder, 44
Snapper, 19
Snapper haddock, 22
Southern flounder, 48
Southern fluke, 48
Southern kingfish, 37
Sow hake, 23
Spadefish, 76
Spanish mackerel, 56
Speckled hind, 15
Speckled trout, 33
Spikes, 51
Spiny dogfish, 63
Spot, 31
Spot bass, 34
Spottail bass, 34
Spotted flounder, 47
Spotted grouper, 16

Spotted jewfish, 16
Spotted sea trout, 33
Squirrel hake, 24
Striped bass, 8
Striper, 8
Summer flounder, 46
Summer trout, 29
Surf whiting, 39
Swell toad, 72
Swordfish, 73

Tacks, 51
Tautog, 71
Tinkers, 51
Tomcod, 26
Tommy cod, 26
Topcat, 80
Trout, 29, 33, 38
Tuna, 51, 53

Virginia mullet, 30, 37

Warsaw, 13
Warsaw grouper, 13
Watermelon tuna, 58
Weakfish, 29
White-eyes, 31
White grunt, 81
White hake, 23
White marlin, 40
White perch, 9
White shad, 49
Whiting, 27, 30, 37, 39
Windowpane, 47
Winter flounder, 43
Winter trout, 33
Wolffish, 69
Wrasses, 70

Yearling drum, 34
Yellowfins, 31
Yellowfin trout, 29
Yellow-mouth trout, 29
Yellowtail, 32

Exciting Hancock House Fishing Titles

Trout Fishing
Ed Rychkun
5 ½ x 8 ½ 120 pp. SC
ISBN 0-88839-317-2

An instant classic. Ed Rychkun provides a sure-fire guide to catching trout. Well thought-out, organized, and illustrated. A rewarding book for both the novice and experienced fisherman.

Mooching:
The Salmon Fisherman's Bible
David Nuttall
5 ½ x 8 ½ 184 pp. SC
ISBN 0-88839-097-1

David Nuttall has not only given a complete and accurate description of the techniques and skills required to become a highly successful moocher, but also has eloquently transmitted the big picture. Mr. Nuttall brings alive the experiences, situations, and feelings of fishing.

Saltwater Salmon Fly-fishing
Barry Thornton
5 ½ x 8 ½ 160 pp. SC
ISBN 0-88839-319-9

Fly fishermen intrigued by the prospect of casting a fly for salmon in the open salt water can find all they need to know in this thorough study of the pastime. Barry Thornton brings his expertise to the reader in masterful form.

Manuscripts Wanted

Hancock House is always looking for good manuscripts. We publish history, natural history, science, and similar titles. Do you or a friend have a book idea? We are not a subsidy publisher—the publication costs are ours and our authors receive royalties.

David Hancock
Publisher